SEVEN LAYERS OF SOCIAL MEDIA ANALYTICS

Seven Layers of Social Media Analytics

Mining Business Insights from Social Media Text, Actions, Networks, Hyperlinks, Apps, Search Engine, and Location Data

Gohar F. Khan

"This is a useful guide to the emerging world of social media analysis. It offers one the first practical frameworks for understanding social media. The volume provides step-by-step instructions for the complete work flow for data collection and analysis, including advanced network science methods. This is a must read for serious analysts seeking to empirically document and optimize social media."—**Marc Smith, Director, Social Media Research Foundation**.

"the seven layers of social media analytics explores the value of analyzing social media data for informing organizational decision making. It provides a 7-step process that is straightforward, showing a way out of the dense and murky impressions from a huge collection of status updates, comments, hyperlinks and other online verbal jungle."—**Gabrielle Iglesias, Knowledge Management & Communication Specialist, Asian Disaster Preparedness Center**.

"Although we are still living in the early years of the digital network revolution, some of its consequences for politics, economics, society and business are already apparent. One of these is the dramatic rise in recent years of social media which, along with the burgeoning Internet of things, are themselves a major source of so-called "big data." For companies, individuals and organizations seeking to find their way in the new communications environment, Gohar F. Khan has provided a very helpful guidebook to the use of social media analytics. It is well organized and clearly written and should help many make sense of this rapidly emerging, increasingly consumer and citizen-centric environment."—**James F. Larson, Professor and Chair, Department of Technology and Society, SUNY Korea**.

"Seven layers of social media analytics provides a fascinating insight into how social media data can be mined for business intelligence purposes. Given the growing importance of social media, this book is highly recommended."-**Jacob Wood, Assistant Professor, Korea University of Technology and Education**.

To my lovely family.
Thank you. Without your support and patience, I would have never completed this book.

The book comes with a companion site (www.7LayersAnalytics.com) which hosts:

- ✓ Up-to-Date Tutorials (with screenshots)
- ✓ Lecture Slides
- ✓ Case Studies
- ✓ Sample Data, and
- ✓ Sample Syllabus.

CONTENTS

ACKNOWLEDGMENTS

I would like to thank the following individuals without whose help this book would never have been completed.

Gabrielle Iglesias, Asian Disaster Preparedness Center

Görkem Çetin, Countly

Hannah Tregear, Customer Marketing Manager, BrandWatch

Intzar Ali Lashari, Mærsk Mc-Kinney, Møller Instituttet, Denmark

Jacob Wood, Assistant Professor, Korea University of Technology and Education

James F. Larson, Professor, SUNY Korea

Lora Wan, Enterprise Development Representative, Hootsuite

Manho Lee, the Seoul Metropolitan Government, South Korea

Marc Smith, Director, Social Media Research Foundation

Rob Ackland, CEO, Uberlink

Ryan Seams, Support Team, Mixpanel

Seth Redmore, VP Marketing, Lexalytics, Inc.

Stuart W. Shulman, CEO, DiscoverText

PREFACE

In the *Seven Layers of Social Media Analytics: Mining Business Insights from Social Media Text, Actions, Networks, Hyperlinks, Apps, Search Engines, and Location Data,* we draw on developments in social media analytics theories and tools to develop a comprehensive seven-layer framework that allows readers to get their minds around how social media data can be used to mine useful business insights. The book offers concepts, tools, tutorials, and case studies that business managers need to extract and analyze the seven layers of social media data, including *text, actions, networks, apps, hyperlinks, search engines, and location layers.* Social media analytics is about converting unstructured social media data into meaningful business insights. By the end of this book, you will have mastered the concepts, techniques, and tools used to extract business insights from social media that help increase brand loyalty, generate leads, drive traffic, and ultimately make good business decisions.

A separate chapter is dedicated to each layer. Here is how the book is structured.

Chapter 1: The Seven Layers of Social Media Analytics—this chapter sets the theme for the rest of the book and introduces the seven layers of social media analytics, discusses the typical steps needed to carry out the analytics, and explains the challenges and tools of social media analytics.

Chapter 2: Understanding Social Media—before diving into the seven layers of social media data, chapter 2 briefly discusses fundamental social media technologies; their properties; and mainstream social media tools, including blogs, wikis, social networking sites, content communities, and folksonomies.

Chapter 3: Social Media Text Analytics—chapter 3 is dedicated to *text analytics*, the first layer of social media analytics. A variety of textual elements of social media are discussed along with the steps needed to carry out text analytics, its purpose, and the tools of text analytics. The chapter also includes a step-by-step guide on analyzing social media text (e.g., tweets and comments) using Semantria for Excel.

Chapter 4: Social Media Network Analytics—networks are fundamental parts of social media. Chapter 4 deals with network analytics and seeks to identify influential nodes (e.g., people and organizations) and their position in the network. Social media networks, such as Facebook, Friendship Network, Twitter, and YouTube are discussed. The chapter also includes a case study and a step-by-step tutorial on NodeXL for analyzing social media networks.

Chapter 5: Social Media Actions Analytics—chapter 5 deconstruct the second layer of social media analytics, that is, the *actions analytics*. The chapter explains extracting, analyzing, and interpreting the actions performed by social media users, such as likes, dislikes, shares, mentions, and endorsement. The chapter also includes a case study and a step-by-step tutorial on Hootsuite's analytical tool.

Chapter 6: Social Media Apps Analytics—mobile applications are the next frontier in the social business landscape. Chapter 6 deals with mobile analytics and marketing issues. A practical tutorial on analyzing and understanding in-app purchases, customer engagement, and demographics are included in the chapter. A practical tutorial on the Countly apps analytics tool and a real-world case study is also included.

Chapter 7: Social Media Hyperlink Analytics—Social media traffic is carried out through the hyperlinks embedded within it, thus hyperlink (e.g., in-links and out-links) analysis can reveal, for example, Internet traffic patterns and sources of the incoming or outgoing traffic to and from a source. Hyperlink analytics is discussed in chapter 7. A real-world case study and step-by-step guidelines on hyperlink analytics using VOSON are also included.

Chapter 8: Social Media Location Analytics—chapter 8 deals with location analytics, which is also known as spatial analysis or geospatial analytics. The chapter outlines tools and techniques to mine and map the location of social media users, contents, and data. A real-world case study on mining mobile phone data and a step-by-step guide on geo-mapping tabular business data using Google Fusion Table is also provided.

Chapter 9: Social Media Search Engines Analytics—this chapter explains search engines analytics. Search engines analytics focus on analyzing historical search data to gain valuable insight into trends analysis, keyword monitoring, and advertisement spending statistics. Practical step-by-step guidelines are provided using Google Trends to analyze search engine data.

Chapter 10: Aligning Social Media Analytics with Business Goals—Configuring and understanding social media tools alone are not enough; to get the most out of it, analytics should be aligned with business strategy. Chapter 10 will discuss strategies and techniques to align social media analytics with business goals. A discussion and framework on social media risk management is also included in the chapter.

CHAPTER 1

SOCIAL MEDIA ANALYTICS: AN OVERVIEW

SOCIAL MEDIA analytics is the art and science of extracting valuable hidden insights from vast amounts of semistructured and unstructured social media data to enable informed and insightful decision making. It is a science, as it involves systematically identifying, extracting, and analyzing social media data using sophisticated tools and techniques. It is also an art, interpreting and aligning the insights gained with business goals and objectives. In order to get value from analytics, one should master both its art and science. The science part of social media analytics requires skilled data analysts, sophisticated tools and technologies, and reliable data. Getting the science right, however, is not enough. To effectively consume the results and put them into the action, the business must master the other half of analytics, that is, the art of interpreting and aligning analytics with business objectives and goals. Interpreting analytics results, for example, requires representing the data in meaningful ways, having domain-specific knowledge, and training. Aligning analytics with business goals is discussed in a later chapter.

Social media analytics is a relatively new but emerging field. Based on Google's trends data (Figure 1), the term *social media analytics* seems to have appeared over the Internet horizon during 2009, and interest in it (in terms of people searching for it) has steadily increased since then. As social media is becoming mainstream and people are using it to express feelings and interests, share content, and collaborate, the social media analytics field is also gaining prominence among both the research and business communities. Businesses need to tap into the vast amounts of data produced by social media users to increase brand loyalty, generate leads, drive traffic, make forecasts, and ultimately make good decisions. Social media data and users are of great value to business. A study, for example, found that the average value of a Facebook fan was $174.17 in key consumer areas (Syncapse 2013). KINAXIS, a supply chain management company, for example, used eighteen employee bloggers and generated over forty-two million leads (Petersen 2012). The case study included at the end of the chapter demonstrates this point and shows how ESPN FC used social media during the World Cup to increase awareness of ESPN FC and to drive football fans to their website for the latest news, scores, and team information, all in an effort to help build the profile of the brand across the globe.

PURPOSE OF SOCIAL MEDIA ANALYTICS

The main premise of social media analytics is to enable informed and insightful decision making by leveraging social media data (Chen, R.H.L. et al. 2012; Bekmamedova and Shanks 2014). The following are some sample questions that can be answered with social media analytics.

- What are customers using social media saying about our brand or a new product launch?
- Which content posted over social media is resonating more with my customers?
- How can I harness social media data (e.g., tweets and Facebook comments) to improve our product/services?
- Is the social media conversation about our company, product, or service positive, negative, or neutral?
- How can I leverage social media to promote brand awareness?
- Who are our influential social media followers, fans, and friends?
- Who are our influential social media nodes (e.g., people and organizations) and their position in the network?
- Which social media platforms are driving the most traffic to our corporate website?
- Where is the geographical location of our social media customers?
- Which keywords and terms are trending over social media?
- How active is social media in our business and how many people are connected with us?
- Which websites are connected to my corporate website?
- How are my competitors doing on social media?

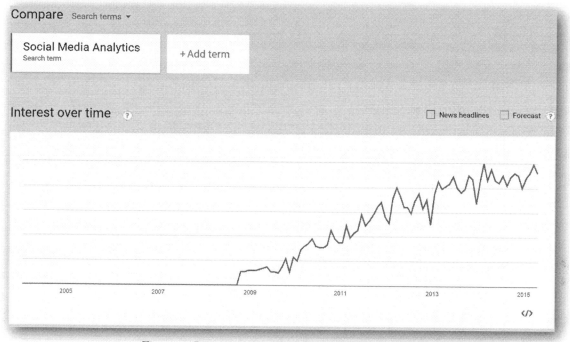

Figure 1. Interest in social media analytics overtime

SOCIAL MEDIA VS. TRADITIONAL BUSINESS ANALYTICS

While the premise of both social media and traditional business analytics is to produce actionable business, they do however slightly differ in scope and nature. Table 1 provides a comparison of social media analytics with conventional business analytics. As an emerging field, it may not be appropriate to use the term *conventional* for business analytics; we do so here for comparison purposes only.

The most visible difference between the two comes from the source, type, and nature of data mined. Unlike the traditional business analytics of structured and historical data, social media analytics involves the collection, analysis, and interpretation of semistructured and unstructured social media data to gain an insight into the contemporary issues while supporting effective decision making (Bekmamedova and Shanks 2014). Social media data is highly diverse, high volume, real-time, and stored in third-party databases in semistructured and unstructured formats. Structured business data, on the other hand, is mostly stored in databases and spreadsheets in machine-readable format (e.g., rows and columns), thus it can be easily searched, computed, and mined. Unstructured and semistructured social media data is not machine readable and can take a variety of forms, such as the contents of this book, Facebook comments, e-mails, tweets, hyperlinks, PowerPoint presentations, images, emoticons, videos, etc. Thus, it is not analytics friendly and needs a lot of cleaning and transformation.

Another visible difference comes from the way the information (i.e., text, photographs, videos, audio, etc.) is created and consumed. Social media data originates from the public Internet and is socialized in nature. Socialized data is a collective good, created and consumed using various social media platforms and social technologies to maintain social and professional ties (e.g., Facebook, LinkedIn etc.), to facilitate knowledge sharing and management (Wikipedia, blogs, etc.), to create awareness (Twitter, etc.), or to exchange information in the form of text, audio, video, documents, graphics, etc. (Khan 2013). Social media data is social, informal, and not bound (i.e., the Internet is a boundary), unlike the conventional analytics data, which is bureaucratic, formal in nature, controlled by organizations, and bound or trapped within the organizational network or intranet. More importantly, the value or impact of socialized data is determined by the extent to which it is shared with other social entities (e.g., people or organizations): the more it is shared (i.e., socialized) the greater its value. For example, the value/effect of information can be measured in terms of attracting more followers (e.g., on Twitter or Facebook), page views or clicks, or in terms of socio-political impact (e.g., information disseminated using social media to organize political or social movements may have more effect in terms of organizing the events). However, the majority of the conventional business data is confined within the organizational databases, limitedly shared, and can serves as a source of competitive advantage.

Table 1. Social media vs. conventional business analytics

Social Media Analytics	Business Analytics
Semistructured and unstructured data	Structured data
Data is not analytical friendly	Data is analytical friendly
Real-time data	Mostly historical data
Public data	Private data
Stored in third-party databases	Stored in business-owned databases
Boundary-less data (i.e., Boundary within the Internet)	Bound within the business intranet
Data is high volume	Data is medium to high volume
Highly diverse data	Uniform data
Data is widely shared over the Internet	Data is only shared within organizations
More sharing creates greater value/impact	Less sharing creates more value
No business control over data	Tightly controlled by business
Socialized data	Bureaucratic data
Data is informal in nature	Data is formal in nature

SEVEN LAYERS OF SOCIAL MEDIA ANALYTICS

Social media at a minimum has seven layers of data (Figure 2). Each layer carries potentially valuable information and insights that can be harvested for business intelligence purposes. Out of the seven layers, some are visible or easily identifiable (e.g., text and actions) and other are invisible (e.g., social media and hyperlink networks). The following are seven social media layers that will be discussed in detail in the subsequent chapters.

1. Text
2. Networks
3. Actions
4. Hyperlinks
5. Mobile
6. Location
7. Search engines

Seven Layers of Social Media Analytics

Layer One: Text

Social media text analytics deals with the extraction and analysis of business insights from textual elements of social media content, such as comments, tweets, blog posts, and Facebook status updates. Text analytics is mostly used to understand social media users' sentiments or identify emerging themes and topics. Chapter 3 is dedicated to social media text analytics.

Layer Two: Networks

Social media network analytics extract, analyze, and interpret personal and professional social networks, for example, Facebook, Friendship Network, and Twitter. Network analytics seeks to identify influential nodes (e.g., people and organizations) and their position in the network. Network analytics are discussed in chapter 4.

Layer Three: Actions

Social media actions analytics deals with extracting, analyzing, and interpreting the actions performed by social media users, including likes, dislikes, shares, mentions, and endorsement. Actions analytics (discussed in chapter 5) are mostly used to measure popularity, influence, and prediction in social media. The case study included at the end of the chapter demonstrates how social media actions (e.g., Twitter mentions) can be used for business intelligence purposes.

Layer Four: Mobile

Mobile analytics is the next frontier in the social business landscape. Mobile analytics deals with measuring and optimizing user engagement with mobile applications (or apps for short). Chapter 6 discusses mobile analytics and provides a practical tutorial on analyzing and understanding in-app purchases, customer engagement, and mobile user demographics.

Layer Five: Hyperlinks

Hyperlink analytics is about extracting, analyzing, and interpreting social media hyperlinks (e.g., in-links and out-links). Hyperlink analysis (discussed in chapter 6) can reveal, for example, Internet traffic patterns and sources of incoming or outgoing traffic to and from a source.

LAYER SIX: LOCATION
Location analytics, also known as spatial analysis or geospatial analytics, is concerned with mining and mapping the locations of social media users, contents, and data. Chapter 7 is dedicated to location analytics.

LAYER SEVEN: SEARCH ENGINES
Search engines analytics focuses on analyzing historical search data for gaining a valuable insight into a range of areas, including trends analysis, keyword monitoring, search result and advertisement history, and advertisement spending statistics. Chapter 7 is dedicated to search engines analytics.

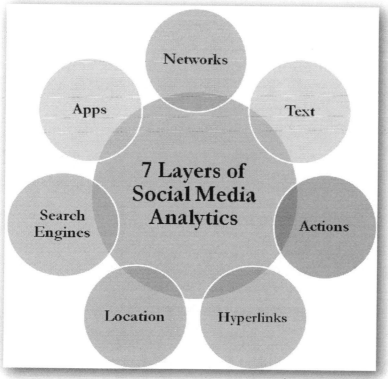

Figure 2. Seven layers of social media analytics

TYPES OF SOCIAL MEDIA ANALYTICS

Like any business analytics, social media analytics can take three forms: 1) descriptive analytics, 2) predictive analytics, and 3) prescriptive analytics.

DESCRIPTIVE ANALYTICS

Descriptive analytics is mostly focused on gathering and describing social media data in the form of reports, visualizations, and clustering to understand a business problem. Actions analytics (e.g., no. of likes, tweets, and views) and text analytics are examples of descriptive analytics. Social media text (e.g., user comments), for example, can be used to understand users' sentiments or identify emerging trends by clustering themes and topics. Currently, descriptive analytics accounts for the majority of social media analytics.

PREDICTIVE ANALYTICS

Predictive analytics involves analyzing large amounts of accumulated social media data to predict a future event. For example, an intention expressed over social media (such as buy, sell, recommend, quit, desire, or wish) can be mined to predict a future event (such as purchase). Or a business manager can predict sales figures based on historical visits (or in-links) to a corporate website. The TweepsMap tool, for example, can help you determine the right time to tweet for maximum alignment with your audience time zone. Or, based on analyzing your social media users' languages, it can suggest if it is time to create a new Twitter account for another language.

PRESCRIPTIVE ANALYTICS

While predictive analytics help to predict the future, prescriptive analytics suggest the best action to take when handling a scenario (Lustig, Dietrich et al. 2010). For example, if you have groups of social media users that display certain patterns of buying behavior, how can you optimize your offering to each group? Like predictive analytics, prescriptive analytics has not yet found its way into social media data.

SOCIAL MEDIA ANALYTICS CYCLE

Social media analytics is a six step irrelative process (involving both the science and art) of mining the desired business insights from social media data (Figure 3). At the center of the analytics are the desired business objectives that will inform each step of the social media analytics journal. Business goals are defined at the initial sage, and the analytics process will continue until the stated business objectives are fully satisfied. To arrive from data to insights, the steps may vary greatly based on the layers of social media mined (and the type of the tool employed). The following are the six general steps, at the highest level of abstraction, that involve both the science and art of achieving business insights from social media data.

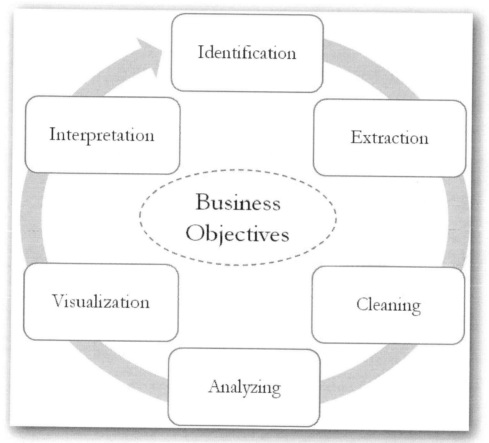

Figure 3. Social media analytics cycle

STEP 1: IDENTIFICATION

The identification stage is the art part of social media analytics and is concerned with searching and identifying the right source of information for analytical purposes. The numbers and types of users and information (such as text, conversation, and networks) available over social media are huge, diverse, multilingual, and noisy. Thus, framing the right question and knowing what data to analyze is extremely crucial in gaining useful business insights. The source and type of data to be analyzed should be aligned with business objectives. Most of the data for analytics will come from your business-owned social media platforms, such as your official Twitter account, Facebook fan pages, blogs, and YouTube channel. Some data for analytics, however, will also be harvested from nonofficial social media platforms, such as Google search engine trends data or Twitter search stream data. The business objectives that need to be achieved will play an important role in identifying the sources and type of data to be mined. Aligning social media analytics with business objectives is discussed in a later chapter.

STEP 2: EXTRACTION

Once a reliable and minable source of data is identified, next comes the science of extraction stage. The type (e.g., text, numerical, or network) and size of data will determine the method and tools suitable for extraction. Small-size numerical information, for example, can be extracted manually (e.g., going through your Facebook fan page and counting likes and copying comments), and a large-scale automated extraction is done through an API (application programming interface). Manual data extraction maybe practical for small-scale data, but it is the API-based extraction tools that will help you get most out of your social media platforms. Mostly, the social media analytics tools use API-based data extraction. APIs, in simple words, are sets of routines/protocols that social media service companies (e.g., Twitter and Facebook) have set up that allow users to access small portions of data hosted in their databases. The greatest benefit of using APIs is that it allows other entities (e.g., customers, programmers, and other organizations) to build apps, widgets, websites, and other tools based on open social media data. Some data, such as social networks and hyperlink networks, can only be extracted through specialized tools.

Two important issues to bear in mind here are the privacy and ethical issues related to mining data from social media platforms. Privacy advocacy groups have long raised serious concerns regarding large-scale mining of social media data and warned against transforming social spaces into behavioral laboratories. The social media privacy issue first came into the spotlight particularly due to the large-scale "Facebook Experiment" carried out in 2012, in which Facebook manipulated the news feeds feature of thousands of people to see if emotion contagion occurs without face-to-face interaction (and absence of nonverbal cues) between people in social networks (Kramer, Guillory et al. 2014). Though the experiment was consistent with Facebook's Data Use Policy (Editorial 2014) and helped promote our understanding of online social behavior, it does, however, raise serious concerns regarding obtaining informed consent from participants and allowing them to opt out.

The bottom line here is that your data extraction practices should not violate a user's privacy and the data extracted should be handled carefully. While all social media platforms have their privacy policies in place, to be on the safe side it is advisable to craft your own social media privacy policy. Your policies should explicitly detail social media ownership in terms of both accounts and activities such as individual and page profiles, platform content, posting activity, data handling and extraction, etc.

STEP 3: CLEANING

This step involves removing the unwanted data from the automatically extracted data. Some data may need a lot of cleaning, and others can go into analysis directly. In the case of the text analytics, for example, cleaning, coding, clustering, and filtering may be needed to get rid of irrelevant textual data using natural language processing (NPL). Coding and filtering can be performed by machines (i.e., automated) or can be performed manually by humans. For example, DiscoverText combines both machine learning and human coding techniques to code, cluster, and classify social media data (Shulman 2014).

STEP 4: ANALYZING

At this stage the clean data is analyzed for business insights. Depending on the layer of social media analytics under consideration and the tools and algorithm employed, the steps and approach you take will greatly vary. For example, nodes in a social media network can be clustered and visualized in a variety of ways depending on the algorithm employed. The overall objective at this stage is to extract meaningful insights without the data losing its integrity. While most of the analytics tools will follow you through the step-by-step procedure to analyze your data, having background knowledge and an understanding of the tools and its capabilities is crucial in arriving at the right answers.

STEP 5: VISUALIZATION

In addition to numerical results, most of the seven layers of social media analytics will also result in visual outcomes. The science of effective visualization known as visual analytics is becoming an important part of interactive decision making facilitated by solid visualization (Wong and Thomas 2004; Kielman and Thomas 2009). Effective visualization is particularly helpful with complex and huge data because it can reveal hidden patterns, relationships, and trends. It is the effective visualization of the results that will demonstrate the value of social media data to top management. Depending on the layer of the analytics, the analysis part will result in relevant visualizations for effective communication of results. Text analytics, for instance, can result in a word cooccurrence cloud; hyperlink analytics will provide visual hyperlink networks; and location analytics can produce interactive maps. Depending on the type of data, different types of visualization are possible, including the following.

Network data (with whom)—network data visualizations can show who is connected to whom. For example, a Twitter following-following network chart can show who is following whom. Different types of networks are discussed in a later chapter.

Topical data (what)—topical data visualization is mostly focused on what aspect of a phenomenon is under investigation. A text cloud generated from social media comments can show what topics/themes are occurring more frequently in the discussion.

Temporal data (when)—temporal data visualization slice and dice data with respect to a time horizon and can reveal longitudinal trends, patterns, and relationships hidden in the data. Google trends data, for example, can visually investigate longitudinal search engine trends (Google trends are discussed in chapter 9).

Geospatial data (where)—geospatial data visualization is used to map and locate data, people, and resources. The chapter on location analytics provides more details on mapping.

Other forms of visualizations include trees, hierarchical, multidimensional (chart, graphs, tag clouds), 3-D (dimension), computer simulation, infographics, flows, tables, heat maps, plots, etc.

STEP 6: INTERPRETATION

Interpreting and translating analytics results into a meaningful business problem is the art part of social media analytics. This step relies on human judgments to interpret valuable knowledge from the visual data. Meaningful interpretation is particularly important when we are dealing with descriptive analytics that leave room for different interpretations. Having domain knowledge and expertise are crucial in consuming the obtained results correctly. Two strategies or approaches used here can be 1) producing easily consumable analytical results and 2) improving analytics consumption capabilities (Ransbotham 2015). The first approach requires training data scientists and analysts to produce interactive and easy-to-use visual results. And the second strategy focuses on improving management analytics consumption capabilities (Ransbotham 2015).

CHALLENGES TO SOCIAL MEDIA ANALYTICS

Social media data is high volume, high velocity, and highly diverse, which, in a sense, is a blessing in terms of the insights it carries; however, analyzing and interpreting it presents several challenges. Analyzing unstructured data requires new metrics, tools, and capabilities, particularly for real-time analytics that most businesses do not possess. Some social media analytics tools are listed in a later section.

VOLUME AND VELOCITY AS A CHALLENGE

Social media data is large in size and is swiftly generated. Capturing and analyzing millions of records that appear every second is a real challenge. For example, on Twitter, three-hundred forty-two thousand tweets appear every minute, and on Facebook, one million likes are shared every twenty minutes. Capturing all this information may not be feasible. Knowing what to focus on is crucial for narrowing down the scope and size of the data. Luckily, sophisticated tools are being developed to handle high-volume and high-velocity data.

DIVERSITY AS CHALLENGE

Social media users and the content they generate are extremely diverse, multilingual, and vary across time and space. Not every tweet, like, or user is worth looking at. A tweet or mention coming from an influential social media user is more important than a tweet from a noninfluential user. Due to the noisy and diverse nature of social media data, separating important content from noise is challenging and time consuming.

UNSTRUCTUREDNESS AS A CHALLENGE

Unlike the data stored in the corporate databases, which are mostly numbers, social media data is highly unstructured and consists of text, graphics, actions, and relations. Short social media text, such as tweets and comments, has dubious grammatical structure, and is laden with abbreviations, acronyms, and emoticons (a symbol or combination of symbols used to convey emotional expressions in text messages), thus representing a great challenge for extracting business intelligence.

SOCIAL MEDIA ANALYTICS TOOLS

To keep up with the growing need for analyzing the vast amount of data, social media analytical tools are also coming to market at a great pace. Social media analytics tools come in a variety of forms and functionalities. Table 2 lists some example tools with respect to each layer of social media analytics. These tools are briefly discussed in their respective chapters. Aligned with your social media strategy, these tools can be used to measure different layers of social media data.

Table 2. Examples of social media analytics tools with respect its layers

Layer of social media	Example of tools
Text	Discovertext Lexalytics Tweet Archivist Twitonomy Netlytic LIWC Voyant
Actions	Lithium Twitonomy Google Analytics SocialMediaMineR
Network	NodeXL UCINET Pajek Netminer Flocker Netlytic Reach Mentionmapp
Mobile	Countly Mixpanel Google Mobile Analytics
Location	Google Fusion Table Tweepsmap Trendsmap Followerwonk Esri Maps Agos
Hyperlinks	Webometrics Analyst VOSON
Research Engines	Google Trends

CASE STUDY: THE UNDERGROUND CAMPAIGN THAT SCORED BIG

BACKGROUND

ESPN is a digital sports leader in the UK, operating websites and apps that deliver a range of multimedia content to sports fans. ESPN.co.uk, the brand's central offering in the region, covers most sports, including football, cricket, rugby, tennis, golf, boxing, F1, and others. Other sport-specific websites under ESPN's stewardship include ESPNcricinfo and ESPN FC, which are available in app form, as is the award-winning ESPN UK app.

With a mandate to serve sports fans wherever they are, whenever they want it, ESPN's websites and apps carry the latest news, live scores, video, tables, fantasy games, and more. Featuring ESPN's global roster of talents from across the entire sporting spectrum, the brand has enjoyed significant growth in the past twelve months in key user engagement metrics, and continues to do so. ESPN is a sports television channel in the United Kingdom and Ireland owned by BT Group under license from American sports broadcaster ESPN Inc.

The channel was operated by ESPN from 2009 to 2013, when it was sold to BT and became part of its BT Sport package focusing on international sporting events, predominantly American sports. Programming is available in standard definition and high definition formats.

ESPN FC is the football-dedicated division of ESPN, providing rolling coverage of the world's most popular sport. Formerly ESPN Soccernet, ESPN FC is a multimedia football website that currently has Global, UK, US, and Spanish editions. The site offers news, live scores, fantasy football, blogs, stats, interactive polls and more, ESPN FC showcases the best in world football coverage. Through ESPN FC TV, the website hosts football-related video, utilizing the brands roster of global football experts, journalists and contributors, providing insight, analysis and reaction to football around the globe.

THE GOAL

The World Cup is the most widely viewed and followed sporting event in the world. The 2014 event, held in Brazil, was an eagerly anticipated event with major sponsorship from some of the largest organizations on the planet, including Adidas, Coca-Cola and VISA. Teams—and fans—from all corners of the earth travelled to the country. The world's spotlight was on Brazil. ESPN FC wanted to capitalize on the mountains of excitement, enjoyment and enthusiasm from people all over the planet to hear about the matches taking place in Brazil.

ESPN FC's main goal over the period of the World Cup was to increase awareness of ESPN FC and to drive football fans to www.espnfc.co.uk for the latest news, scores and team information, helping build the profile of the brand across the globe.

THE CHALLENGE

ESPN FC likes to go the extra mile to serve sports fans, anytime and anywhere. With the World Cup being held outside the UK, many of the games were being played at inconvenient times for sports fans in the UK to watch them live on TV, as the matches were being played while people were still at work, travelling home, or very late in the evening. ESPN FC wanted to find a way to get the games to sports fans wherever they were during the World Cup.

THE SOLUTION

During the World Cup 2014, ESPN FC estimated that 100 million people would travel on the London Underground. The majority of London's Underground stations do not have Internet access, meaning fans were kept in the dark with no access to the scores during vital points in the tournament. With their mantra of 'serving sports fans anytime and anywhere,' ESPN FC had the ingenious idea of bringing the results of World Cup games to those travelling on the London Underground. Transport For London (TFL) are a local government body responsible for most aspects of the transport system in Greater London. ESPN FC partnered with TFL to display game results on announcement boards at 150 stations across London—a media first. No brand had ever displayed messages on TFL's boards before.

INFLUENCING THE RIGHT DEMOGRAPHIC

The ESPN FC & TFL World Cup campaign was aimed at the commuting masses. However, ESPN FC wanted to ensure that they were also reaching the specific demographic segments relevant to their brand. Using the Brandwatch (one of the world's leading social media listening and analytics technology platforms) Demographic feature, ESPN FC were able to identify which mentions about the campaign were from Sales, Marketing and PR professionals, a key audience they were attempting to target. In terms of all positive sentiment about the campaign 18% came from Sales, Marketing and PR professionals, and just 0.4% of negative sentiment came from that industry. Those tweets went on to help influence five other important people in that sector, each with over 1,000 followers. Using Brandwatch, ESPN FC were able to measure that those five tweets alone reached nearly 15,000 followers.

UNDERGROUND RESULTS

Searching for the online reception of a campaign when there is no Internet reception can be tricky. Using Brandwatch, ESPN FC tracked 3,438 online mentions of the campaign in the first 7 days. This figure is of course limited due to the fact that most commuters have no access to Wi-Fi or Internet whilst on the London Underground, but indicative of the residual engagement of the campaign and the fact that so many remained excited about the campaign when returning to street level—enough to share it online. "of the mentions relating to the live coverage over 60% of them were positive a figure much higher than for most marketing campaigns." Charles Boss, Head of Marketing, ESPN FC UK. In order to truly understand the effectiveness of this campaign, ESPN FC used Brandwatch Analytics to measure how many mentions other London Underground-based projects received over a similar time frame. Remarkably, the recent decision to introduce Euro cash points in London tube stations generated only 218 mentions in the first week, whilst commuters mentioning Virgin Media's new London Underground Wi-Fi was only slightly better with 473 mentions over 7 days. When placed in this context, ESPN FC's World Cup updates were mentioned over 7 times more than these similar campaigns, proving they had the loudest fans and the campaign was well received.

THE RIGHT LINE

Finding out where commuters are tweeting can be just as important as what they are tweeting. ESPN FC utilized Brandwatch's advanced Boolean Queries to listen to conversation specifically from each tube line during the campaign. The Central Line proved to generate the largest volume of conversation of ESPN FC's World Cup updates, with 40% of tweets coming from that line, whereas the Northern and Jubilee lines followed with 27% and 23% of the chat. These insights could prove to be invaluable to ESPN FC when planning future social media advertising campaigns on the London Underground. As, Charles Boss, Head of Marketing, ESPN FC UK put it, "…Brandwatch was able to demonstrate that, using their Impression score, the campaign reached a potential 2,363,921 people on Twitter…"

COMMENTATING TO COMMUTERS

During the campaign, London commuters travelling during the World Cup final were able to follow Germany's 1–0 win over Argentina thanks to ESPN FC's live commentary and analysis at Waterloo Station. The game was relayed over the public address system at London's busiest train station by ex-Chelsea defender Scott Minto and Tottenham Hotspur Assistant Head Coach Steffen Freund. Using Brandwatch's sentiment analysis ESPN FC was able to gauge public reaction during the commentary. Of the mentions relating to the live coverage over 60% of them were positive, a figure much higher than for most marketing campaigns. More significantly, ESPN FC didn't receive a single negative mention for their World Cup Final commentary: pretty impressive considering many of those commuting during football's signature game aren't the biggest fans of the sport.

Source: Brandwatch, *www.brandwatch.com*

Review Questions

1. Why it is important for business managers to understand and mine social media data?
2. What is social media analytics, and how it is different from traditional business analytics?
3. Briefly explain the seven layers of social media data. Support your answer with examples.
4. Explain the social media analytics cycle.
5. What ethical issues should be considered when mining social media data?
6. What are some main challenges to social media analytics?
7. Compare different social media analytics tools available in the market and explain their strengths and weakness.

CHAPTER 2

INTRODUCTION TO SOCIAL MEDIA

Social media is becoming an integral part of life in contemporary society and has changed the creation, sharing, and consumption of information. There are countless stories related to the role of social media in contemporary society, either in the entertainment industry where it propelled Psy (a Korean rapper) to worldwide fame through the spread of his "Gangnam Style" YouTube video, or in political landscape during the period commonly called the "Arab Spring" or "Facebook revolution."

Diffusion and use of social media in contemporary society is noteworthy. Billions of people are flocking to social media platforms, such as Facebook, Twitter, and YouTube, where they share, tweet, like, and post content. Social media growth, tools, and big data also present unparalleled opportunity to market products, enhance brand loyalty, network with customers, crowd-source ideas, drive sales, and mine business insights. Before diving into each layer of social media analytics, let's look at some common types of social media and their underlying tools and technologies.

WORLD WIDE WEB

At the very core of social media is the World Wide Web (WWW) and the Internet. The Internet is the global network of interconnected devices, such as personal computers, smartphones, switches, routers, satellites, and cables. It is composed of several technologies, and one of the underlying software technologies is the WWW, or simply, "the web." The web in its simplest form is composed of interlinked hypertext documents (i.e., websites) that can be accessed through web browsers (Berners-Lee 1993) such as Internet Explorer and Chrome. The web has drastically evolved since it was first created. The earliest version is referred to as Web 1.0.

Web 1.0

Web 1.0, or "read-only web," was an early version of the web. Web 1.0 was and is static in nature; that is, it allows only one-way information flow in a one-to-many fashion. Web developers and designers would create websites and content for users to consume. The design of the website could not allow users to contribute content or respond to it; hence, Web 1.0 users were only passive recipients of the information/content. In that sense, Web 1.0 was yet another channel of one-way information distribution like any other conventional one-to-many technologies, such as radio and television. Web 1.0 websites were only used for information presentation purposes, and not for generating information or content.

Web 2.0

Web 2.0 totally altered the WWW landscape by turning the web into a collaborative ecosystem where users can an actively create content, share ideas, and cocreate products and services. Unlike the early version of the web, Web 2.0 allows two-way and many-to-many information flow and user-generated content (Oreilly 2007; Kaplan and Haenlein 2010; Kietzmann, Hermkens et al. 2011). The content generated by users over social media platforms is known as user-generated content (UGC). Some tools of this collaborative ecosystem are podcasting, blogging, tagging, social bookmarking, social networking, wikis, and other collaborative tools (the social media tools are discussed later in this chapter). One important thing to note is that Web 2.0 is not a technical standard or an update to the early standard (i.e., Web 1.0), but it reflects the changes in the way people use the web (or programmers design the websites). Somehow (perhaps due to changing societal norms), the webmasters and programmers decided to give more control to users by letting them present as well as generate content.

Web 3.0

Web 3.0 is the next revolution in the WWW and will alter the web yet again. In addition to having the properties of Web 2.0, Web 3.0 will mark the era of a connected web operating system where most software components (e.g., application programs and operating systems) and data processing will reside on the web. The Web 3.0 will be smarter, quicker, and more reliable in connecting data, concepts, applications, and people. An important dimension of the Web 3.0 is the Semantic Web, or linked data. The Semantic Web is known as the "web of data"(W3 2015) and aims to make huge amounts of data (and the relationship among the datasets) web-available in a machine-readable format (such as Resource Description Framework [RDF] format) so that it can be queried by applications. RDF is a general-purpose language for representing information on the web (W3 2015).

SOCIAL MEDIA

Built on the Web 2.0 philosophy (i.e., give more control to the user over the content), social media is an easy-to-use Internet-based platform that provides users with opportunities to create and exchange content (such as text, videos, audio, and graphics) in a many-to-many context. *Social media* and *Web 2.0* are often use interchangeably, but they can be slightly differentiated (Kaplan and Haenlein 2010). At the core of social media is the Web 2.0 concept, and social media can be considered an application of the Web 2.0 concept. In other words, social media is realized based on the Web 2.0 concept.

One important thing to note is that social media is not limited only to the well-known platforms such as Facebook, Twitter, YouTube, and blogs. In this book, we consider as social media any online platform (proprietary or purpose built) that enable users to participate, collaborate, create, and share content in a many-to-many context.

CORE CHARACTERISTICS OF SOCIAL MEDIA

The best way to understand social media is through its core characteristics that set it apart from the conventional medium. All these properties play an important role in creating a collaborative ecosystem.

SOCIAL MEDIA IS MANY-TO-MANY

Social media enables interaction among the users in a many-to-many fashion. This is unlike conventional technological media such as print, radio, telephone, and television.

SOCIAL MEDIA IS PARTICIPATORY

Unlike conventional technologies, social media encourages participation and feedback from users. Social media users can participate in online discourse through blogging, comments, tagging, and sharing content.

Seven Layers of Social Media Analytics

Social Media Is User Owned

While social media platforms are provided by corporations (such as Google and Facebook), the content is generated, owned, and controlled by social media users. Without the user-generated contents and active involvement from the users, social media would be empty, boring online spaces.

Social Media Is Conversational

It is not only the ease of conversation but also the many-to-many conversation abilities that make social media stand out from the traditional one-to-one or one-to-many medium of interaction. The many-to-many conversation characteristics of social media make it possible for the masses to communication and collaborate in real time.

Social Media Enables Openness

Social media provides new opportunities to access data and information through Web 2.0 channels.

Social Media Enables Mass Collaboration

Social media channels allow masses to collaborate in a many-to-many fashion to achieve certain shared goals.

Social Media Is Relationship Oriented

Most social media tools allow users to easily establish and maintain social and professional relationships and ties. Some social media tools, such as Facebook, are solely focused on personal relationships, whereas others, such as Twitter, are focused on professional relationships.

Social Media Is Free And Easy to Use

Being free and easy to use are two of the reasons that social media has proliferated in such a space.

TYPES OF SOCIAL MEDIA

Broadly speaking, based on authentication or access mechanisms, social media tools are available in two forms: 1) Internet-based, and 2) smartphone-based. Internet-based social media platforms are generally accessed through e-mail IDs. Facebook, LinkedIn, Cyworld, and Google+ are examples of Internet-based social media. Note that an Internet-based social media platform can also be accessed through any device connected to the Internet, including a smartphone application (or app for short), but the authentication mechanism is still the same. Whereas, smartphone-based social media platforms are accessed through mobile phone numbers; that is, users can only log in using mobile phone numbers. KaKao Talk, Tender, and 1KM are the popular example of phone-based social network services. These application can only installed and accessed from a phone; for example, in its current form, one cannot use KaKao Talk, 1KM, or Tender through a personal computer. Mobile applications are also an example of mobile-based social media tools (mobile applications are discussed later).

Below, we briefly discuss different social media tools and how businesses can leverage them.

SOCIAL NETWORKING SITES

Social networks sites or services (SNS) are types of social media platforms that are solely focused on online social relationships among users. Some examples of SNS include Facebook, Google+, and Cyworld. SNS allow users to build and maintain social relationships among people who share interests, activities, backgrounds, or real-life connections. Most SNS allow "users to (1) construct a public or semipublic profile, (2) establish links (friendship) and relationships with other SNS users, and (3) view and traverse their list of connections and those made by others within the system." (Boyd and Ellison 2007) (p. 1–2). Currently, there are two versions of SNS, a publically available and a business SNS. For example, in addition to its public version, Facebook recently announced releasing a business social networking site, "Facebook at Work," aimed at cooperate users and allowing them to create social networks and collaborate.

USING FACEBOOK FOR BUSINESS PURPOSES

Founded in 2004 by Mark Zuckerberg, Facebook is an online social network service or site where users can create profiles; upload photos and video; send messages; and keep in touch with friends, family and colleagues. As of May 2013, Facebook had more than 1.11 billion registered users. Apart from its primary function as an online social network site, Facebook has become an important marketing and outreach channel for all sorts of organizations including governments.

How can business benefit from Facebook? The answer is Facebook pages or fan pages. Fan pages can serve as excellent advertisement and networking channels with your customers. Facebook fan pages are a great way to connect and network with customers. The following questions may bring some clarity and focus to your Facebook fan page efforts.

✓ What is the purpose of the Facebook page? And is the purpose aligned with your business goals?
✓ Who will be responsible for handling your Facebook page (e.g., posting information, responding to comments and complaints)?
✓ What should be your Facebook page name?
✓ What information should be posted and what should not be posted?
✓ Do you have a legal mandate to establish an official Facebook page for your organization?
✓ Do you have a plan to collect and analyze feedback generated over your Facebook page?
✓ What are your security measures from possible online risks?

CONTENT COMMUNITIES

Content communities, such as YouTube and Flicker, are defined[1] by "a group of people coalescing online around an object of interest held in common. The object can be just about anything for example, photos, videos, links, topic or issue, and is often organized and developed in a way that either includes social network elements or makes them central to the content." The most popular content community site is YouTube.

USING YOUTUBE FOR BUSINESS PURPOSES

YouTube is a video-sharing website on which users can upload, view, and share videos. It was created in February 2005 and has been owned by Google since late 2006. An important feature of YouTube is the YouTube channel. A YouTube channel is a public online

---

1   Source: Technology in Prevention, "Content Communities." Available from http://technologyinprevention.wikispaces.com/Content+Communities.

space (or page) on YouTube. A YouTube channel allows you to upload videos, leave comments, or make playlists. Businesses from around the world use YouTube channels in a variety of ways. For example, it is a great way to advertise, educate customers by uploading training materials, awareness videos, information about your product and services. Khan Academy (https://www.khanacademy.org/) is a great example of the effective use of educational videos on YouTube.

Before configuring a YouTube channel, the questions raised in the previous section should be reviewed and answered. Answers to most of the questions should be rooted in your social media strategy

- ✓ What is the purpose of the YouTube channel? (e.g., advertisement promotes awareness, share useful content, provide training etc.) And is the purpose aligned with your business goals?
- ✓ Who will be responsible for handling the channel (e.g., creating and posting videos)?
- ✓ What should be the name of your channel?
- ✓ What type of content should be posted and what should not be posted?
- ✓ Do you have a legal mandate to establish an official YouTube channel for your organization?
- ✓ Do you have a plan to collect and analyze feedback generated over the channel?
- ✓ How will you secure your channel from possible online risks?

BLOGS

A blog is a type of online personal space or website where an individual (or organization) posts content (text, images, videos, and links to other sites) and expresses opinions on matters of personal (or organizational) interest on a regular basis. The most popular blogging platforms are http://www.wordpress.com and http://www.bloggers.com. Mostly, blogging does not require technical know-how or programming skills, so ordinary users can easily build and manage a professional-looking blog.

BLOG FEATURES

Important features of a blog include:

Interactivity—Readers have the ability to leave comments in response to a blog post.

Archives—Blogs provide archives of past blog entries stored in reverse chronological order (that is, the most recent appears first).

Subscription—Internet users can subscribe to blogs. Subscribed users are alerted when new content is posted on the blog.

Focused—Most blogs are focused on a certain area of interest.

Using Blogs for Business Purposes

An official business blog is not just a business diary or journal, but a great way to build a community of readers and receive early and direct feedback on business issues and solicit innovative ideas. As with other platforms, before creating your business blog, review the following questions.

- ✓ What is the purpose of the official blog? (e.g., advertisement promotes awareness, solicit ideas.) And is the purpose aligned with the business goals?
- ✓ Who will be responsible for handling the blog (e.g., creating and posting content)?
- ✓ What should be the name of your blog?
- ✓ What type of content should be posted and what should not be posted?
- ✓ Do you have a legal mandate to establish an official blog for your organization?
- ✓ Do you have a plan to collect and analyze feedback generated over the blog?
- ✓ How will you secure the blog?

Microblogging

Microblogging is a miniature version of blogging that allows users to exchange/publish brief messages, including text, images, or links to other websites. The most popular microblogging platform is Twitter.

Twitter is an online microblogging service that enables users to send and read short messages commonly known as "tweets." A tweet is a text message limited to one hundred forty characters. Let's spend some time to understand basic Twitter terminologies.

Tweet

A tweet is a one hundred forty-character message posted via Twitter. You can also include links and pictures in a tweet.

Retweet (RT)

A retweet is a reposting of someone else's tweet or message. One way to gauge the popularity of your tweets is by measuring retweets. Popular tweets get reposted many times.

Direct messages

Unlike a tweet, which is public and seen by everyone, a direct message is a personal tweet (like e-mail) seen only by the sender and the recipient. However, a direct message can only be sent to people following you.

Following

Following is how you subscribe to other people over Twitter. On Twitter, following someone means that:

- You are subscribing to their tweets as a follower (their tweets will appear on your Twitter main page).
- Their updates will appear in your Home tab.
- That person is able to send you direct messages.

Followers

Followers are people who follow you over Twitter. If someone follows you it means that:

- They will show up in your followers list.
- They will see your tweets in their home timeline whenever they log in to Twitter.
- You can send them direct messages.

Research suggests that the number of followers and following strongly correlated, meaning that people who follow more people get more followers vise versa. One of your objects over Twitter is to increase your flowers.

Mention

When another user includes your username preceded by the @ symbol in a tweet, it is called a "mention." Your Mentions tab (on the Notifications page) collects tweets that mention you by your username so you can keep track of conversations others are having with you. Number of mentions is an indication of influence or popularity.

Hashtags (#)

The hashtag (#) symbol is used to mark keywords or topics in a tweet. It is an easy way to categorize messages. Clicking on a hashtagged word in any message shows you all other tweets marked with that keyword.

USING TWITTER FOR BUSINESS PURPOSES

Twitter is a great way to keep your customers informed. Businesses from around the world use Twitter to keep customers informed by disseminating news and information almost in real time. Setting up Twitter is a very simple process. However, it should not be taken lightly, as the Twitter channel will officially represent your organization. Before proceeding to setup, do a little bit of planning. The following question may bring some clarity and focus to your Twitter efforts.

- ✓ What is the purpose of the Twitter account? And is the purpose aligned with your business goals? Your social media strategy will determine the main purpose of using Twitter or any other social media platform.
- ✓ Who will be responsible for handling it? Since it is not a one-shot deal, once a social media presence is established, it needs to be sustained and managed properly
- ✓ What should be your Twitter handler or username? Be thoughtful while creating a handle; think of a name that truly sums up your organization.
- ✓ What information should be posted and what should not be posted? Your departmental information or communication policy may provide a useful place to start.
- ✓ Do you have legal mandate to establish a Twitter account?
- ✓ Do you have a plan to collect and analyze feedback generated over Twitter?
- ✓ How will you secure your account from online security risks?

ONLINE COLLABORATIVE PROJECTS

Wikipedia is an example of online collaborative projects. Online collaborative projects/ tools allow people to plan, coordinate, add, control, and monitor content in collaboration with others. At the core of the online collaborative projects is the concept of wiki. A wiki is a type online content management system that allows users to add, modify, or delete content simultaneously in collaboration with others. Famous examples of wiki-based platforms are Wikipedia and wiki-spaces. The concept of wiki was first conceived by Ward Cunningham.

USING WIKIS FOR BUSINESS PURPOSES

Wikis are a great way to communicate and collaboratively work on projects with other people. A good example of collaborative wiki is http://www.wikipedia.com. Wikipedia has more than thirty million articles in 287 languages written collaboratively by volunteers around the world. However, Wikipedia is just one type of website built on the wiki model. There are several other notable wikis. Google (www.sites.google.com) provides project wikis that can be configured for business purposes. The questions discussed in earlier sections should be reviewed before configuring a business wiki.

FOLKSONOMIES OR TAGGING (E.G., DEL.ICIO.US)

The term folksonomy, also known as social tagging, social indexing, and collaborative tagging, is attributed to Thomas Vander Wal. The word was created by fusing *folk* and *taxonomy*. In simple words, it is the method of organizing data and content (through tagging) from a user's perspective. For example, del.icio.us, a social bookmarking system, allows users to tag, organize, classify, and share content (web addresses or sites) in their own unique ways. These days, almost all prominent companies (e.g., Facebook and Flicker) also provide tagging services to their users. Since the contents are tagged with useful keywords, social tagging expedites the process of searching and finding relevant content.

VIRTUAL WORLDS

Virtual worlds is computer-generated online environments. It can take the form of a three-dimensional (3-D) virtual social world (e.g., Second Life) where people digitally represent themselves in the form of avatars and interact with others through text and voice messaging. It can also take a form of virtual interactive games, such as World of Warcraft. Mostly, the virtual world environment is created by the users themselves. Virtual reality is another dimension of virtual worlds, where real and virtual are fused together. Virtual reality uses computer software and hardware tools to simulate physical presence the virtual world.

MOBILE APPS

Mobile apps are becoming an integral part of our lives. Mobile apps are special-purpose tools developed to perform a variety of activities we do every day while on the move, such as communicating, social networking, sharing information, and shopping. Tender and Skout, for example, are designed to facilitate social relations, and Viber is designed to facilitate communication. Detailed discussion on apps is provided in a later chapter.

PURPOSE-BUILT PLATFORMS

Social media is not only limited to the aforementioned types, but any online platform (including purposely built in-house platforms) that enable us to participate, collaborate, create, and share content in a many-to-many context can be called social media. Content can be anything, including information, audio/video, profiles, photographs, text, etc. Organizations are increasingly creating purpose-built social media platforms for inter-organizational collaboration activities. A good example of such a platform is the Enterprise 2.0, (McAfee 2006) which uses social media tools (such as blogs, wikis, and group messaging software) to allow employees, suppliers, and customers to network together and share information.

Review Questions

1. Differentiate among Web 1.0, Web 2.0, and Web 3.0.
2. What is social media? And what makes it different from the traditional media?
3. What are some core characteristics of social media?
4. Briefly explain different social media types with examples.
5. Briefly explain how businesses can leverage Facebook, YouTube, Twitter, blogs, and wikis?
6. Differentiate among social media, Web 2.0, and social network sites.

CHAPTER 3

SOCIAL MEDIA TEXT ANALYTICS

TEXT IS one of the fundamental elements of the social media platforms. Textual elements of social media include comments, tweets, blog posts, product reviews, and status updates. Social media text analytics, also known as text mining, is a technique to extract, analyze, and interpret hidden business insights from textual elements of social media content. Organizations use text analysis techniques to extract hidden valuable meaning, patterns, and structures from the user-generated social media text for business intelligence purposes. Text analytics, for example, is useful in gaining a quick and accurate understanding of the emotion and sentiment expressed over social media channels (e.g., tweets or Facebook comments) related to a brand or a new product launch. The case study included in the chapter demonstrates this point and shows how Flyertalk.com successfully mined the textual feedback that their current and potential customers provide in their website. The volume and speed at which the comments over social media are generated does not allow for manual reading, and calls for advanced text analysis techniques. Text analytics has evolved into a well-established field with roots in variety of domains, including data mining, machine learning, natural language processing, knowledge management, and information retrieval. Studies have suggested that approximately 80 percent of data in an organization is textual in nature; in this book, however, we only focus on social media text analytics.

TYPES OF SOCIAL MEDIA TEXT

Based on its nature, social media text can be broadly classified into two categories: 1) dynamic text and 2) static text.

DYNAMIC TEXT

Dynamic text is a real-time social media user-generated text or statement to expresses an opinion about content or information posted over social media. Dynamic text is mostly posed by social media users in response to social, political, economic, personal, cultural, or business issues to express their views and feelings related to it. Dynamic text is usually smaller in length (e.g., a couple of sentences), diverse in nature, and is updated or deleted more frequently. Examples of dynamic social media text include tweets, Facebook comments, and product reviews. Below, we briefly explain the two most common dynamic social media texts: tweets and comments.

Tweet

A tweet is a one hundred forty-character massage posted by a Twitter user. A tweet may include text, images, video, or links to other websites. A tweet may also include a hashtag (#). Hashtags are used to mark keywords or topics in a tweet, and are organically created by Twitter users as a method to categorize messages. A keyword marked by a hashtag can easily appear in Twitter search, and popular hashtags are often trending topics over Twitter. Tweets accumulate over time, carry a time stamp and user information, and mostly appear in descending order; that is, the most recent first. Tweet data provides a valuable source for mining value business insights, including exploring trending topics, measuring brand sentiment, and gathering feedback on new products and services.

Comments

Social media comments are written (usually short) statements that express opinions about content or information posted over social media. While most comments are text only, it can also include images, video, or links to other websites. The ability to post comments and participate in social media discourse is the underlying characteristic that distinguishes social media from traditional media (e.g., TV and print). Like tweets, social media comments are also a great source for mining valuable business insights from social media. Almost all social media platforms provide commenting features. Comments accumulate over time, carry a time stamp and user information, and mostly appear in descending order; that is, the most recent first.

Discussion

Discussion takes the form of textual or written conversation or debate about a certain topic, product, or service. Mostly, discussions among social media users happen through Internet forums. Internet discussion forums are treelike in structure; that is, a forum can contain a number of sub-forums focused on specific topics or threads. In these forums users can post questions and reply to questions posted by other users. Discussions accumulate over time, carry a time stamp and user information, and mostly appear in descending order; that is, the most recent first. Vault Network is an example of an Internet forum that focuses on online games.

Conversation

Social media textual conversation (also known as chatting) is an instant exchange of short written messages between two more people. Chatting usually takes a casual form and are carried out through dedicated messaging services/tools. A variety of messaging tools have been developed for textual conversation, including desktop-based (e.g., Skype); web-based (e.g., Google Hangouts and Facebook chat) and mobile-based (e.g., Viber). Note that these services are not only limited to textual conversation, but also support video and voice conversation. And now that all media are converging, most of the messaging services also come in desktop, mobile, and web forms. For example, Skype has both desktop and Smartphone versions. An important point to note here is that most of the social media textual conversation is private in nature and may not be subject to mining.

Reviews

Reviews are critical evaluations of a product or service performed by customers and experts. They can take both longer and shorter forms. Reviews by customers are mostly shorter when compared to formal reviews by experts. Reviews can include textual elements and ratings. ProductReview.com.au, for example, is a site devoted to product/service reviews and ratings submitted by customers. Product reviews can serve as an excellent source for mining customers' opinions and feelings about a product or service.

STATIC TEXT

Static social media text is usually large in length (e.g., several paragraphs) and is generated, updated, or deleted less frequently. Examples of static text include wiki content, a blog page, Word documents, corporate reports, electronic mail (e-mail), and news transcripts. At the highest level of abstraction, the purpose of static social media text is to inform, educate, and elaborate.

PURPOSE OF TEXT ANALYTICS

Both dynamic and static text are subject to analytics. The following are some of the objectives of social media text analytics for business intelligence purposes (Figure 4).

SENTIMENT ANALYSIS

Sentiment analysis analyzes and categorizes social media text as being positive, negative, or neutral. Social media sentiment analysis mostly focuses on dynamic text. The primary purpose of sentiment analysis is to determine how your customers feel about a particular product, service, or issue. For example, as a product manager, you might be interested to know how your customers on Twitter feel about a product/service that was recently launched. Analyzing your tweets or Facebook comments may provide an answer to your question. Using sentiment analysis, you may be able to extract the wordings of the comments and determine if they are positive, negative, or neutral. At the end of the chapter, several analytical tools are listed for semantic analysis. A later section in the chapter provides a step-by-step guide on analyzing social media text using Semantria.

Semantria is an example of a text sentiment analysis tool. It will go through the following steps to extract sentiments from a document:

Step 1: It breaks the document into its basic parts of speech, called POS tags, which identify the structural elements of a sentence (e.g. nouns, adjectives, verbs, and adverbs).

Step 2: Algorithms identify sentiment-bearing phrases like "terrible service" or "cool atmosphere."

Step 3: Each sentiment-bearing phrase earns a score based on a logarithmic scale ranging from negative ten to positive ten.

Step 4: Next, the scores are combined to determine the overall sentiment of the document or sentence. Document scores range between negative two and positive two. For example, to calculate the sentiment of a phrase such as "terrible service," Semantria uses search engine queries similar to the following:

"(Terrible service) near (good, wonderful, spectacular)"
"(Terrible service) near (bad, horrible, awful)"

Each result is added to a hit count; these are then combined using a mathematical operation called "log odds ratio" to determine the final score of a given phrase.

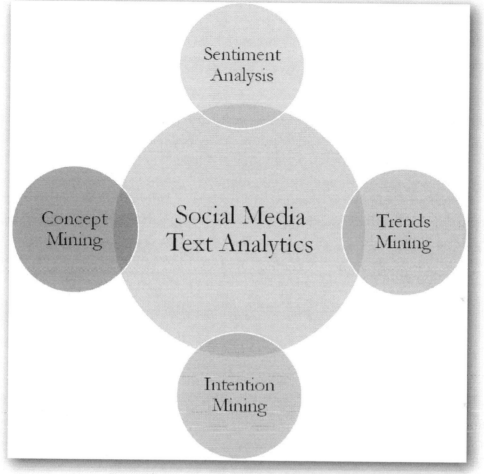

Figure 4. Purpose of social media text analytics

INTENTION MINING

Intention or intent mining (Chen, Lin et al. 2002) aims to discover users' intention (such as buy, sell, recommend, quit, desire, or wish) from natural language social media text such as user comments, product reviews, tweets, and blog posts. Social media as the integral part of our contemporary lives and is widely used by millions of customers to express desires, needs, and intention (Niven 2013). Companies may use intent mining to find new potential customers who intend to buy a product (or services) and service existing customers who have trouble with a product. For example, an analysis of company-related tweets may detect purchase intention based on the presence of the word "buy" or "purchase." Similarly, detecting the "quit" intention may identify and service the customers at risk of leaving the company. The Semantria analytical tool discussed later in this chapter, for example, can be used to mine intentions.

TRENDS MINING

Trends mining, also known as predictive analytics, uses huge amounts of historical and real-time social media data to predict future events. For example, a vast amount of social media data (e.g., comments and tweets) can be mined to identify patterns and trends for new product or service development or to improve customer satisfaction by anticipating their needs. Trend mining exploits patterns in large amounts of data by using sophisticated statistical techniques, including machine learning, data mining, and social network analysis. Predictive analysis using conventional business data has been used in a variety of domains, including marketing, banking, telecommunication, and healthcare. However, social media predictive analytics is still an emerging practice and may take some time for sophisticated tools and techniques to emerge.

CONCEPT MINING

Concept mining aims to extract ideas and concepts from documents. Unlike text mining, which is focused on extracting information, concept mining extracts ideas from large document sets. Thus, concept mining is useful in extracting ideas from large amounts of static social media text, such as wiki content, a web page, Word documents, and news transcripts. Concept mining can be employed to classify, cluster, and rank ideas.

STEPS IN TEXT ANALYTICS

Text analytics, like any other form of social media analytics, is the art and science of getting the desired business intelligence from the text posted over social media (Figure 5). While the steps required for text analytics are largely dependent on the type of approach and tool employed, a typical social media text analysis includes the following cyclical steps.

IDENTIFICATION AND SEARCHING

The text analytics process starts with identifying the source of the text that will be analyzed. Text posted on social media is dynamic, huge, diverse, multilingual, and noisy. Thus, finding the right source for the purpose of text analytics is very crucial for gaining useful business insights. The genre of the source text also will determine the type of tool used to extract and analyze it. For example, extracting tweets requires different tools and approaches than analyzing a document or website text. Analyzing tweets, for example, requires API-based searching and extraction of data from the Twitter timeline based on criteria that you specify. You can choose to extract tweets that include specific keywords, such as your company name. The desired business question that needs to be answered with text analytics will serve as a good starting point.

TEXT PARSING AND FILTERING

The next step is to parse, clean, and filter the text, and create a dictionary of words using NPL, which is mostly based on machine learning techniques. In order for computer and algorithms to extract meanings from the text, the sentence structures and parts of speech are determined, named entities extracted (people, organizations, product/service names, etc.), stop words removed, and spellings are checked. Most of these steps are automatic; however, in certain stages, human intervention is required. For example, in the filtering stage, manually cleaning (by humans with domain expertise) may be required to remove unwanted or irrelevant terms.

TEXT TRANSFORMATION

For analytical algorithms to be applied to the text, it should be transformed into a computer-readable format (e.g., 0s and 1s) for analysis. The cleaned text is thus transformed into numerical representations using linear algebra-based techniques, such as latent semantic analysis and vector space models.

TEXT MINING

At this step, the text is actually mined to extract the needed business insights. Varieties of text mining algorithms are applied to the text, such as clustering, association, classification, and predictive analysis, and sentiment analysis. Text analysis employs these sophisticated algorithms to extract sentiment and meanings from the text in a similar manner to the way human do; however, the process is thousands of times faster.

Association—Association or association mining is a data-mining technique used to determine the probability of the cooccurrence of items in a collection of documents. The relationships between cooccurring items are expressed as association rules. In text analytics, for example, social media text can be clustered together based on cooccurrence frequency. Or it can be used, for example, to find that a user who liked a social media content A and B is 90 percent likely to also like content C.

Clustering—Clustering or cluster analysis groups objects based on similarity in non-overlapping groups. Clustering is an important part of data mining and text analytics. Social media text (such as tweets or comments), for example, can be clustered into positive, negative, and natural categories. Or nodes in a social media network can be clustered based on importance.

Classification—From the text analytics perspective, classification or categorization is used to find similarities in the document and groups them with predefined labels based on the themes contained in the document (Chakraborty, Pagolu et al. 2013). For example, an e-mail can be classified as spam based on its contents.

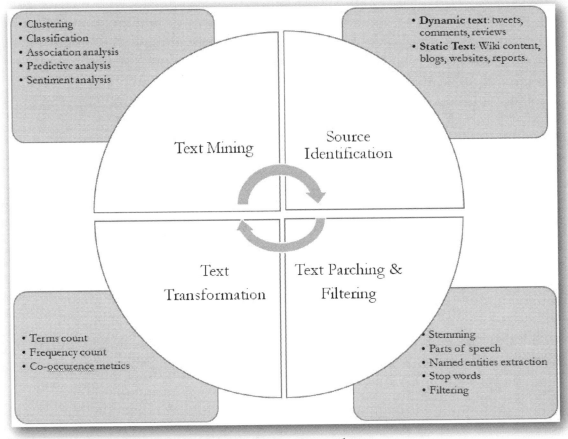

Figure 5. Steps in text analytics

SOCIAL MEDIA TEXT ANALYSIS TOOLS

A variety of social media text analysis tools are available on the market. Some are free and others are paid. Below we list some popular text analysis tools.

Discovertext: Discovertext (http://discovertext.com/) is a powerful platform for collecting, cleaning, and analyzing text and social media data streams.

Lexalytics: Lexalytics (http://www.lexalytics.com/) is a social media text and semantic analysis tool for social media platforms, including Twitter, Facebook, blogs, etc.

Tweet Archivist: Tweet Archivist (https://www.tweetarchivist.com/) is focused on searching, archiving, analyzing, and visualizing tweets based on a search term or hashtag (#).

Twitonomy: Twitonomy (https://www.twitonomy.com/) is a Twitter analytics tool for getting detailed and visual analytics on tweets, retweets, replies, mentions, hashtags, followers, etc.

Netlytic: Netlytic (https://netlytic.org) is a cloud-based text and social network analytics platform for social media text that discovers social networks from online conversations on social media sites.

LIWC: Linguistic Inquiry and Word Count (LIWC) is a text analysis tool for analyzing emotional, cognitive, structural, and process components present in individuals' verbal and written speech samples: http://www.liwc.net/

Voyant: Voyant (http://voyant-tools.org/) is a web-based text reading and analysis. With Voyant, a body of text can be read from a file or directly exported from a website.

CASE STUDY: TAPPING INTO ONLINE CUSTOMER OPINIONS

BACKGROUND

Founded in 1986, Frequent Flyer Services (Flyertalk.com) has created a unique niche for itself within the travel industry as a company that conceives, develops and markets products and services exclusively for the frequent traveler. Its focus and distinctive competency lie in the area of frequent traveler programs. Worldwide, these frequent traveler programs in the airline, hotel, car rental and credit card industries have more than 75 million members who earn an excess of 650 billion miles per year.

The Problem

Flyertalk.com is one of the most highly trafficked travel domains. It features chat boards and discussions that cover the most up-to-date traveler information, as well as loyalty programs for both airlines and hotels. With millions of user generating millions of posts and comments, it wanted to tap into the explosion of customer opinions expressed online. Flyertalk.com knew that the feedback that current and potential customers provide on their website provides a rich source of feedback and was looking for ways to mine it.

Solution

The answer to problem faced by Flyertalk.com lies in the text analytics. The most innovative companies know they could be even more successful in meeting customer needs, if they just understood them better. Text analytics is proving to be an invaluable tool in doing this. Flyertalk.com leveraged Anderson Analytics do the job. Anderson Analytics, a full-service market research consultancy, tackles this issue using cutting-edge text analytics and data mining software from SPSS that allows the application of linguistic, statistical and pattern recognition techniques to extremely large text data sets.

Note that the text analytics techniques applied in this case are not limited to discussion boards or blogs but can be applied to any text data source, including survey open ends, call center logs, customer complaint/suggestion databases, e-mails, and social media data, etc.

A text analytics project is usually part of a much larger data mining project that would typically involve the identification of some core strategic questions, the allocation of resources and the eventual implementation of findings. However, the focus of this case study is to describe the tactical aspects of a text analytics project and to delineate the three basic steps involved in text analytics:

Step 1: Data Collection and Preparation
Step 2: Text Coding and Categorization
Step 3: Text Mining and Visualization

STEP 1: DATA COLLECTION & PREPARATION

Having quality data in the proper format is usually more than half of the battle for most researchers. For those who can gain direct access to a well-maintained customer database, the data collection and preparation process is relatively painless. However, for researchers who want to study text information that exists in a public forum such as FlyerTalk.com, data collection can be more complex and usually involves web scraping.

Web scraping (or screen scraping) is a technique used to extract data from websites that display output generated from another program. There are many commercially available applications that can scrape a website and turn the blogs or forum messages into a data table. Here is how Web Scraping works.

Web Scraping Process

Crawl

- Crawl the website and scrape for topic, ID and thread initiator.

Download

- Use topic ID from the first step as part of the URL query string to download messages.

Store

- Web crawl and store message display pages.

Screen Scrape

- Screen scrape stored web pages and extract data into a structured format.

Link

- Link extracted posts with topics from the first step, along with other extracted fields to create the final dataset.

Even with the availability of powerful web-scraping tools and techniques, text mining a popular blog or a message board like the one at FlyerTalk.com presents unique data collection and processing challenges. The amount of free text available on such sites usually prohibits an indiscriminate approach to data scraping. A strategy with clear objectives and a well-defined data extraction method are needed in order to increase the reliability of data analysis in the latter stages of the research.

In this particular case, researchers at Anderson Analytics narrowed the scope to just discussion topics within a 12-month period (from August 2005 to August 2006) on the five major forums intended for discussing the hotel loyalty programs of Starwood, Hilton, Marriott, Inter Continental, and Hyatt hotels.

Specific web-scraping parameters differ depending on the structure of the target sites. In a discussion board format, the text data tend to follow a simple hierarchy. Typically, each forum contains a list of topics, and each topic consists of numerous posts. Therefore, the web-scraping process of FlyerTalk.com initially retrieves data such as the discussion topics, topic ID, topic starter, and topic start date. Then, by using the topic ID, the web-scraping application constructs and submits query strings to the FlyerTalk.com site to retrieve messages associated with each specific topic.

A good web-scraping tool should allow the capture of information that exists in the source data of an html page, not just the displayed text. Therefore, hidden information such as the topic ID, date stamp, etc. also becomes available to the researcher.

Besides making sure the fields in the final dataset are in the correct format, another problem unique to discussion board text needs to be addressed. It is very common for posters to quote others' text within their own posts. These quotes should typically be extracted from the message field and placed in a separate field so as to prevent double counting and inadvertently weighting certain posts.

In addition to the text messages posted on the forum, the web-scraping process should also capture the poster's ID and 'handle' as well as any other available poster information such as forum join date and forum registration information (in this case: location, frequent traveler program affiliation, etc.

STEP 2: TEXT CODING & CATEGORIZATION

Text coding and categorization is the process of assigning each text data record a numeric value that can be used later for statistical analysis. Text coding can apply either dichotomous codes (flags & many variables) or categorical codes (one variable for an entire dataset). Short answers to an open-ended survey question typically use categorical codes. However, the amount of text included in most discussion board posts typically requires dichotomous codes. A typical text coding process has the following steps.

Text Coding & Categorization Process

Preliminary Coding

- Use both computer and human coder to obtain the preliminary understanding of the data.

Initial Classification

- Use SPSS Text Mining tool to perform initial categorization on a sample data set (1/100 of the entire dataset).

Computer Classification

- Information and knowledge gained from the initial concept extraction is used by human coder to assist in computer categorization.

Coding & Classification Refinement

- Categorization and coding are an iterative process. Custom libraries are created to refine the process. Text extraction is performed multiple times until the number of and the details of categories are satisfactory.

Coding & Extraction Rules

- Once the coding result becomes satisfactory, the same coding and extraction rules are used on the entire dataset.

Categorization Results

- Categorization results are exported for further analysis with tools such as SPSS Text Analysis.

Text coding is usually an iterative process. This is particularly true for coding messages on a site such as FlyerTalk.com. This is because compared to survey answers; the text information from discussion boards tends to be less focused. The text data on most discussion boards tend to be "user-driven" rather than "provider-driven."

Before creating categories, researchers at Anderson Analytics first randomly examine a sample of text messages to gain a basic understanding of the data. This step is required to understand the type of acronyms, shorthand and terminologies commonly used on the forum of interest.

SPSS Text Analysis for Surveys and Text Mining for Clementine are powerful tools. However, the text coding results can be greatly improved if the programs can be "trained" to better understand text information particular to the industry and topics of interest.

With a list of industry specific themes, concepts and words, the researchers at Anderson use tools such as SPSS Text Analysis for Surveys to create a custom dictionary. Then the SPSS text analytics applications can be used, in conjunction with an SPSS developed dictionary, to extract highly relevant concepts from the text data.

In this case, examples of some of the basic concepts in the messages that can be detected by the software include: 'rates,' 'stay,' 'breakfast,' 'points,' 'free offers.' The text extraction and categorization processes are repeated with minor modification each time to fine tune results.

STEP 3: TEXT MINING, VISUALIZATION, AND INTERPRETATION

Depending on the needs of any given research project, the coded text data can be interpreted in many different ways. In this case, the data is examined via the following methods:

Positive/Negative comments and overlapping terms

The Flytalk.com data indicate that negative discussions among the posters are centered on the payment process, condition/quality of the bathroom, furniture, and the check in/out process. The praises seem to be centered on topics such as spa facility, complimentary breakfasts, points and promotions.

Data patterns within different hotel brands

By comparing the coded text data of Starwood and Hilton forums, the researchers find that the posters seem to be relatively more pleased with beds on Starwood's board, but more pleased with food and health club facilities on Hilton's board.

Longitudinal data patterns

As this study contains data from a one year period, data can be analyzed to understand how topics are being discussed on a month-to-month basis. The data in this particular case revealed that the discussion about "promotions" on the Starwood board was particularly frequent on February 2006. Cross-checking with Starwood management confirmed that special promotions were launched during that time period. This demonstrates one way to measure the impact of various communication strategies, promotions and even nonplanned external events.

Analysis of Poster Groups

Web mining may be helpful in understanding the aggregate motivation of some of the most active users of the products. Though it may be difficult to segment posters with only one post, frequent posters can provide a relatively rich set of segmentation variables. In this case, some general motivational themes found were the need for being 'in the know,' 'finding deals,' and the desire to "give back."

CONCLUSION

Companies have found that they can compete far more effectively if they gain a true, 360 ° view of their customers. The feedback that current and potential customers provide in blogs, forums and other online spaces provides a rich source of feedback. Using text analytics to monitor this information helps organizations gauge customer reaction to products and services and, when combined with analysis of "structured" transactional data, delivers predictive insight into customer behavior.

This case described how text analytics was applied to information posted by users of travel and hospitality services; but the same techniques can be applied to other industries. A company might find, for example, that when it launches a special promotion, customers mention the offer frequently in their online posts.

Text analytics can help identify this increase, as well as the ratio of positive/negative posts relating to the promotion. It can be a powerful validation tool to complement other primary and secondary customer research and feedback management initiatives. Companies that improve their ability to navigate and text mine the boards and blogs relevant to their industry are likely to gain a considerable information advantage over their competitors.

Source: Anderson Analytics, LLC. *www.andersonanalytics.com*

Tutorial: Text Analytics with Semantria

Introduction

Lexalytics is a text analytics company founded in 2003. They have two products, Salience (an on-premises text analytics engine), and Semantria, a SaaS, API, and Excel plug-in for text analytics. In this tutorial we will configure and use Semantria for Excel for text analytics purposes. Semantria uses text and sentiment analysis techniques to analyze tweets, Facebook comments, surveys, and product reviews. This tutorial assumes that you are using MS Windows 7, Chrome browser, and MS Excel 2010 thirty-two-bit versions. For text analysis purposes, we will use Trip Advisor's sample XLS dataset. The sample dataset contains customer comments extracted from the Trip Advisor website. You can download the XLS file to your computer from Semantria's website: https://semantria.com/support/excel/ or from the book companion website (www.7layersanalytics.com). Create a folder on your computer (e.g., text analytics) and save the file into it. Before starting with Semantria, go to http://www.semantria.com/signup to get a free account.

Getting Started

Semantria requires two pieces of software to run.

- ➤ Windows XP or higher
- ➤ Microsoft Office Excel

Installing Semantria is easy.

1. Go to http://semantria.com/excel and click on the download button.
2. Select your version of Excel to download the installer file.
3. Open it up when it finishes downloading.
4. Click on "Run" to activate the installer.
5. If you haven't registered for Semantria yet, there's a link you can use to register for your free account: If you've already registered, click on "Install" to begin.
6. Click "Next."
7. Read through and accept the license agreement.

8. Click "Next" again.
9. Choose your destination folder.
10. Click "Next" once more.
11. Click "Install."
12. Click "Finish."
13. Finally, click "Close" to exit the installer.
14. Start up Microsoft Excel.
15. Create a new project.
16. Click on the Semantria's ribbon and then Click on "Application Settings" button available at the top right corner (Screenshot 1).

Screenshot 1. Semantria for Excel

17. Input your API and API Secret, which you can find in your registration e-mail.
    a. Make sure to leave no spaces at the beginning or ending of your credentials when copying and pasting from the registration e-mail.
18. Click "Login" and you're now ready to use Semantria for Excel.

After this, download the sample Bellagio Hotel dataset available at: semantria.com/excel/tutorial (the dataset is also available at the book companion site). This is a survey of a hundred reviews from Trip Advisor and will act as our example for this tutorial.

- Mac users: If you are using Parallels to run Windows, save all datasets downloaded from the web onto your Windows-side desktop. You'll need to open these datasets manually in your Windows-side Excel. Opening them directly from the Internet defaults you to Mac OS-side Excel, which will not work.

RUNNING AN ANALYSIS

In order to run our first analysis, we'll follow these steps:

1. Open Excel.
2. Find and open the file "Semantria Bellagio Sample Data Set.xls."
3. You should be presented with four columns: **ID**, **Room Number**, **Customer Name** and **Text** (Screenshot 1).

Screenshot 2. sample data loaded in Semantria

4. Before you do anything else, click the button labeled "Manage Analysis and Reports" on the top left and then click on "New."
5. For the purposes of this tutorial, we want to make sure that "Discover" is selected instead of "Detailed." This will give us a high-level overview of the data.
6. Let's label the analysis as "Bellagio2," and, because the reviews are in English, we'll leave the default language as English.
   You'll see a small button that looks like this ▣ beside the text field for "Select source text." Click it. This will allow you to manually select the source text.
7. Highlight all one hundred reviews by dragging your mouse around them. Click "OK" once you've done this.

8. Now let's analyze this data. A box will appear labeled "Start Analysis," and in it will be the analysis name ("Discovery"), the configuration (English) and the source text selected (Cells B2 to B101). It will tell you "100 documents were found from the selected range." Now click on the "Analyze" button.

9. Look right now at the box labeled "Semantria for Excel." A yellow band will appear with your analysis information contained in it, and it will say "Receiving…" under the heading "Created."

10. Once your analysis is received, the band will turn green and the date of the analysis' creation will appear. Double-click anywhere on this green band, and it will open up a new worksheet. This might take a moment to load. You're now viewing your analysis workbook.

UNDERSTANDING YOUR ANALYSIS

We'll look at four major components of the structured data you're now looking at. First, you'll see the Source Text listed in Column A. To the right of this column is what we'll be paying attention to.

a. **Facets Column**

Each facet is a word that occurred often in your data. We can see that "room" occurred fifty times, "hotel" thirty-five times, and "staff" twenty-nine times. These are the three most common words in our data. Also note how many times each mention of these words was positive, negative, and neutral.

b. **Attribute Column**

Attributes are adjectives that are associated with a facet. So "room" has five facets here, including "nice," "clean," and "lovely." It looks as though people are pretty happy with the rooms. This is confirmed by the low number of negative facets.

c. **Themes Column**

Themes are noun phrases taken from individual comments, and contain the main ideas of your content. To clarify, noun phases are a word or group of words that function in a sentence as subject, object or prepositional phrase. In this case, we find that many of the Themes are somewhat positive: "nice rooms," "excellent food," etc.

d. **Entities Column**

Entities are mostly proper nouns, like people, places, dates, companies, brands, and more. They're usually used to monitor what people are saying about your company—or your competitor's. In this dataset, most of the entities revolve around Las Vegas, the Hotel Bellagio, or Bellagio competitors like the MGM Mirage.

2. All of these components are also represented in graph form automatically via Discovery Mode. Here are examples of what these graphs look like (Screenshot 3).

DETAILED ANALYSIS

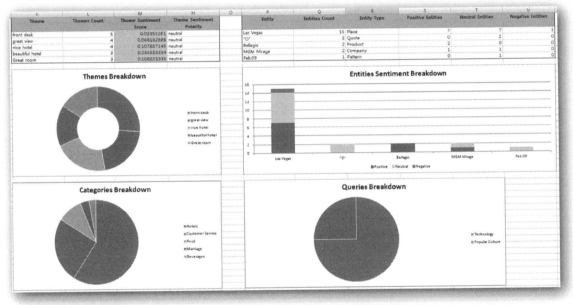

Screenshot 3. Semantria detailed analysis report

Detailed analysis analyzes comments on an individual or "granular" level. Open the Manage Analysis and Reports tab, and click on "New."

1. Select "Detailed."
2. Name this project "Bellagio Detailed."
3. Leave the configuration as "Default English."
4. Select the source text.

5. Highlight all of the reviews and click "OK."
6. Click "Analyze."
7. Now, click the button "Phrases."
8. Double-click on the bar when it turns from yellow to green in the box labeled "Semantria for Excel." You've now opened the detailed analysis for the data in a new worksheet.
9. Notice that every comment has a unique ID.
10. Semantria will assign each ID automatically, although you can assign IDs manually. The source text is the original data we analyzed—the Bellagio reviews from Trip Advisor. You'll see that the first review listed has a document sentiment score of –0.32, therefore this review is negative.
11. The document sentiment score is the score for the review as a whole. This score is made up of various sentiment-bearing phrases in the document, which are all weighted differently depending on the sentence. "Rude," "overpriced," "inefficient"—all of the phrases in this review are negative. Each phrase is given its own sentiment score. This contributes to the overall document sentiment score.
12. You can add phrases or adjust sentiment scores for any Semantria configuration by going into "Sentiment Settings."

Semantria can also pick up on negators and intensifiers if they're used with phrases. It's important to note that a document sentiment score can be neutral, but contain both positive and negative phrases. Scroll down to row 49 for an example of a neutral review that contains both positive and negative feedback. This is why it's important to analyze the reviews on a granular level. Entities and themes are also assigned their own sentiment score. Entities extract the proper noun from each review and assign them their own sentiment score. Look at row 14. Semantria knows that "Las Vegas" is a place, and that in this review it's referred to positively.

Themes are noun phrases that provide the sentence with meaning using lexical chaining technology. Reading through the themes is a great way to figure out what the document is about without having to read it. Look at row 13—"Excellent food." We know the writer of this review had a good experience with the food just by looking at a few words.

Semantria has three methods of categorizations: 1) Auto Categories 2) User Categories and 3) Queries. **Auto Categories** will take your content and map it against over five thousand categories that Wikipedia uses to classify their own articles. **User Categories** is a similar Wikipedia-based classifier that allows you to create your own categories. **Queries** allows you to classify your document using common Boolean operators. Another benefit to the overview capabilities in Discovery mode is the graphs created automatically for **Themes**, **Entities**, **User Categories**, and **Queries**. These are pictured below:

CREATING A USER CATEGORY

Creating a User Category is a way of automatically categorizing your data using the semantic knowledge from Wikipedia.

1. Click on "Manage Categories."
2. Click on "New."
3. Name this category "Customer Service" and give it a default weight of "1."
4. Click "Create."
5. Scroll through the list under the box "Manage Categories" and find the category labeled "Customer Service." Click on this.
6. Now scroll down to the user category sample section.
7. Click "New."
8. Category samples are the words Semantria uses to make reference to Wikipedia. As such, we want to jot down a few words that are related to customer service at a hotel.
9. Clicking "Create" after each one, jot down "customer service," "staff," and "manager." (Screenshot 4).

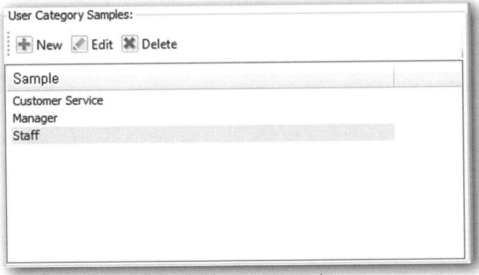

Screenshot 4. new users categories

10. Let's now click on the "Manage Analyses and Reports" tab with the Semantria logo on it.
11. In the right hand pane, click the "Reprocess" button and click "Yes" when prompted.
12. Once the analysis is done processing, we can open it up and sort the reviews to see which ones are about customer service.

Understanding and Creating Queries

You might've noticed the word "rude" appeared three times as a negative attribute for the facet "staff" in our analysis. This is valuable information to know! If you were running the Bellagio, you'd want to know what those reviews said, so that's what we're going to do.

1. Queries is the most specific classifier of the three. Queries are phrases that are searched against in the Semantria service. They're created using "Boolean" syntax—that means you can use "AND," "OR," "NOT," and a few others like "WITH" and "NEAR." Let's learn how to create one.
2. Log in to online.semantria.com
3. Click "Create empty configuration," type "Bellagio3" in the box, and click "Create."
4. Click the "EN Bellagio3" dropdown menu in the upper left (just below the Semantria logo), and select "Queries."
5. Enter a name for the query in the box where it says "query name." Call it "staff."
6. Click on the box right below ("type + [enter] to add terms…"), type "personnel," and hit "Enter" on your keyboard.
7. Now type "staff" in the same box as you put "personnel" and click "Enter." Now you have a query with two terms!
8. Click "Save." (This saves it while you make edits, but doesn't publish it.)
9. Click "Go Live." This makes your configuration active and applies it to your future analyses.

Utilizing VLookup

You can pull data from your original worksheet and add it to any Semantria analysis using the VLookup function. This is useful for deriving additional insight from your data. For example, if you analyze the Bellagio reviews to see which ones had negative sentiment, you can use VLookup to see which room numbers are associated with these negative sentiment reviews. This would show you if many negative reviews are coming from the same room.

1. Open up the "Manage Analysis and Report" tab.
2. Start a new analysis by clicking the "New" button.
3. Select "Detailed" and name this analysis "VLookup."
4. Input the source text with the and select all of the reviews by dragging your mouse as you did before.
5. Now we'll give a unique ID to each review by pressing the same button, , but this time beside the "Optional ID" text field.
6. Now drag the mouse over all cells in column A.
7. Each document must have a unique ID to use the VLookup feature.
8. Now let's run our analysis by clicking the button labeled "Analyze." Wait as we did before for the bar in the right pane to turn from yellow to green.
9. Double-click the bar labeled "VLookup" as soon as it turns green. This will give us our Semantria output.
10. Now if we want to pull the room numbers to this new Semantria output (Column A), we'd drag the mouse and select the whole column, right click, select "Insert → New Column," and label it "Room Number."
11. Now click on cell A3 and input the "=" sign and select" VLookup."
12. Next click on the unique ID cell of the first review (cell B3).
13. "B3" will appear next to "VLookup" in cell A3. Add a comma after "B3."
14. Now click back to the original worksheet tab at the bottom.
15. By dragging your mouse, select the entire table of the original worksheet.
16. In order to lock everything, we'll put dollar signs ($) in front of the cells in the top-center text field.
17. Add a comma and after it put the number "2," because we're extracting information from the second column in our original table.
18. Close the table and hit "Enter."
19. Close the brackets in the text field and hit enter.
20. You should be in the VLookup tab once again. You'll see the room number associated with the original negative complaint now listed in cell A3.
21. Simply double-click the bottom right-hand corner of this cell to apply the formula to the entire column.

ID	Source Text	Detected Language	Detected Language Strength	Document Sentiment	Document Sentiment +/-	Entity	Entity Type	Entity Sentiment	Entity Sentiment +/-	Entity Sentiment Evidence	Theme	Theme Sentiment	Theme Sentiment +/-
fc627784-	Bad experience. Very	English	72	-0.5381188	negative						inefficient	2.4000001	negative
fc627784-	Bad experience. Very	English	72	-0.5381188	negative						rude staff	-1.2	negative
fc627784-	Bad experience. Very	English	72	-0.5381188	negative						unconsistent	-0.9063	negative
fc627784-	Bad experience. Very	English	72	-0.5383188	negative						Bad experience	-1.8680001	negative
fc627784-	Bad experience. Very	English	72	-0.5381188	negative								
fc627784-	Bad experience. Very	English	72	-0.5381188	negative								
27e080c3-	I there went 1 week in	English	108	0.60413176	positive						good condition	0.66000003	positive
27e080c3-	I there went 1 week in	English	108	0.60413176	positive						played blackjack	0.53628001	positive
27e080c3-	I there went 1 week in	English	108	0.60413176	positive						big luxury	0.66000003	positive
27e080c3-	I there went 1 week in	English	108	0.60413176	positive						excellent food	0.60000002	positive
27e080c3-	I there went 1 week in	English	108	0.60413176	positive						good week	0.5	neutral
07da1f7a-	It was a really nice	English	70	0.46810192	positive	Las Vegas	Place	1.67602992	positive	7	little class	0.86993682	positive
07da1f7a-	It was a really nice	English	70	0.46810192	positive						nice hotel	0.86000001	positive
07da1f7a-	It was a really nice	English	70	0.46810192	positive						great effort	0.60000002	positive
07da1f7a-	It was a really nice	English	70	0.46810192	positive						good level	0.5	neutral
07da1f7a-	It was a really nice	English	70	0.46810192	positive						hotel guests	0.51585615	positive
7d51a760-	The Bellagio is an	English	47	0.47628573	positive	Las Vegas	Place	0.51880002	positive	6	absolute haven	-0.1368571	neutral
7d51a760-	The Bellagio is an	English	47	0.47628573	positive						excellent	0.60000002	positive
7d51a760-	The Bellagio is an	English	47	0.47628573	positive						hotel restaurants	0.23157144	neutral
7d51a760-	The Bellagio is an	English	47	0.47628573	positive						reasonably sane	0.63440001	positive
177ed72d-	My stay at the Bellagio	English	74	0.51666671	positive	Las Vegas	Place	0	neutral	1	wonderful	0.80000001	positive
177ed72d-	My stay at the Bellagio	English	74	0.51666671	positive						dining	0.25833336	neutral

Screenshot 5. Text analysis results

BUILDING NESTED QUERIES

Building a nested query is a way to combine multiple query strings into one query. Let's build one.

1. Click on the "Manage Queries Button" in the top bar.
2. In the right pane, click "New."
3. Let's build a query labeled "Poor."
4. In the text field labeled "Query," let's write down the following using Boolean logic: "poor OR rude OR bad."
5. Now click "Create."
6. Let's create one more called "Service."
7. In the Query text field, we'll use the same Boolean logic, this time jotting down: "service OR staff OR manage."
8. We'll also add an asterisk, or "wild card."
   a. Semantria uses a wild card to make reference to an existing Query.
9. Click "Create."
10. To start our Nested Query, let's create one more Query labeled "Poor Service."
11. Under the new Query text field, we'll key in an open bracket "(," a wild card, the name of the Query we want to reference ("Poor") and close of the bracket. We'll now insert an "AND" operator and repeat the process for "Service," so it looks like this: (*Service).

12. Keep in mind it is case sensitive, so if you spelled "poor" with a lower case "p" then continue using that lower case "p" for the entire process.
13. You can only use the "AND" and "OR" operators when using Nested Queries.
14. Click "Create," and now we have a Nested Query.
15. We'll now process the data set by clicking back to the "Manage Analyses and Reports" button in the top menu. Click "New" and select "Detailed" for the analysis mode.
16. Let's call the analysis "Nested."
17. Click the "Source Text" button, , and select the entire D column (D2-D101).
18. Click the "Analyze" button.
19. Now scroll over to "Queries" (column W) and click on the dropdown menu, clicking off all check boxes except "Poor Service."
20. Click off of "Poor Service" from this dropdown menu and onto anything else, depending on the Query output you wish to see.
21. Semantria tags these Queries as "Poor Service," but it will also let us know which Sub-Queries were tagged as well.

Conclusion

This tutorial serves to illustrate an array of basic and advanced uses for the Semantria Excel plugin. While its abilities exceed this tutorial, these are some of its most common and useful features. More information is available elsewhere on the web, including Semantria online support and a variety of other tutorials.

Review Questions

1. What is text analytics, and why it is useful?
2. Differentiate between static and dynamic social media text.
3. Discuss different social media texts.
4. Explain the four main purposes of social media text analytics.
5. Explain the typical social media text analysis steps.

CHAPTER 4

SOCIAL MEDIA NETWORK ANALYTICS

NETWORKS ARE the building blocks of social media and can carry useful business insights. Social media network analytics thus deals with constructing, analyzing, and understanding social media networks. Social network analytics can be used for variety for purposes. It can be employed to identify influential nodes (e.g., people and organizations) or their position in the network, or to understand the overall structure of a network. An organization may mine their Twitter or Facebook follower networks to identify influential network leaders and empower them. People occupying central positions in social media networks are of great value to social marketers, as they have the ability to propagate information to vast numbers of people and are considered opinion leaders. A tweet by President Barack Obama, for example, can instantly reach 48.4 million people. A researcher may be interested in the overall structure of networks to see how certain networks differ or converge. The case study included in this chapter highlights the usefulness of social media networks and how they can be used to answer interesting real-world research questions. The case study shows that how a research team used social media data and proved that the differences in cultural norms (e.g., those of the United States and Korea) influence social media–use patterns in the public sector. Overall, the purpose of network analysis is to (Perer and Shneiderman 2008).

- ✓ Understand overall network structure; for example, number of nodes, number of links, density, clustering coefficient, and diameter.
- ✓ Find influential nodes and their rankings; for example, degree, betweenness, and closeness centralities.
- ✓ Find important links and their rankings; for example, weight, betweenness, and centrality.
- ✓ Find cohesive subgroups; for example, pinpointing communities within a network.
- ✓ Investigate multiplexity; for example, analyzing comparisons between different link types, such as friends vs. enemies.

Common Network Terms

Let's look at some common network terms.

Network

At a very basic level, a network is a group of nodes that are connected with links (Wasserman and Faust 1994). Nodes (also known as vertices) can represent anything, including individuals, organizations, countries, computers, websites, or any other entities. Links (also known as ties, edges, or arcs) represent the relationship among the nodes in a network. Networks can also exist among animals.

Social Networks

A social network is a group of nodes and links formed by social entities where nodes can represent social entities such as people and organizations. Links represent their relationships, such as friendship and trade relations. Social networks can exist both in the real and online worlds. A network among classmates is an example of real world social network. And a Twitter follow-following network is an example of an online social media network. In a Twitter follow-following network, nodes are the Twitter users, and links among the nodes represents the follow-following relationship (i.e., who is following whom) among the users. The subject of this book is online social networks.

Social Network Site

A social network site is a special-purpose software (or social media tool) designed to facilitate the creation and maintenance of social relations. Facebook, Google+, and LinkedIn are examples of social network sites. Different forms of social networks are discussed in a later section.

Social Networking

The act of forming, expanding, and maintaining social relations is called social networking. Using social network sites, users can, for example, form, expand, and maintain online social ties with family, friends, colleagues, and sometimes strangers.

SOCIAL NETWORK ANALYSIS

Social network analysis is the science of studying and understanding social networks (Hanneman and Riddle 2005) and social networking. It is a well-established field with roots in a variety of disciplines including Graph Theory, Sociology, Information Science, and Communication Science.

COMMON SOCIAL MEDIA NETWORK TYPES

The following are some everyday types of social media networks that we come across and that can be subject to network analytics.

FRIENDSHIP NETWORKS

The most common type of social media networks are the friendship networks, such as Facebook, Google+, and Cyword. Friendship networks let people maintain social ties and share content with people they closely associate with, such as family and friends. Nodes in these networks are people, and links are social relationships (e.g., friendship, family, and activities).

FOLLOW-FOLLOWING NETWORKS

In the follow-following network, users follow (or keep track of) other users of interested. Twitter is a good example of follow-following network where users follow influential people, brands, and organizations. Nodes in these networks are, for example, people, brands, and organizations, and links represents follow-following relations (e.g., who is following whom). Below are two common Twitter terminologies.

Following—Following are the people who you follow on Twitter. Following someone on Twitter means:

- You are subscribing to their tweets as a follower.
- Their updates will appear in your Home tab.
- That person is able to send you direct messages.

Followers—Followers are people who follow you on Twitter. If someone follows you, it means that:

- They will show up in your followers list.
- They will see your tweets in their home timeline whenever they log in to Twitter.
- You can send them direct messages.

FAN NETWORK

A fan network is formed by social media fans or supporters of someone or something, such as a product, service, person, brand, business, or other entity. The network formed by the social media users subscribed to your Facebook fan page is an example of a fan network. Nodes in these networks are fans, and links represent colikes, cocomments, and coshares.

GROUP NETWORK

Group networks are formed by people who share common interests and agendas. Most social media platforms allow the creation of groups where member can post, comment, and manage in-group activities. Examples of social media groups are Twitter professional groups, Yahoo Groups, and Facebook groups. Nodes in these networks are group members, and links can represent cocommenting, coliking, and coshares.

PROFESSIONAL NETWORKS

LinkedIn is a good example of professional networks where people manage their professional identify by creating a profile that lists their achievements, education, work history, and interests. Nodes in these networks are, for example, people, brands, and organizations, and links are professional relations (such as coworker, employee, or collaborator). An important feature of professional networks is the endorsement feature, where people who know you can endorse your skills and qualification.

CONTENT NETWORKS

Content networks are formed by the content posted by social media users. A network among YouTube videos is an example of a content network. In such a network, nodes are social media content (such as videos, tags, and photos) and links can represent, for example, similarity (content belonging to the same categories that can be linked together).

DATING NETWORKS

Dating networks (such as match.com and Tender) are focused on matching and arranging a dating partner based on personal information (such as age, gender, and location) provided by a user. Nodes in these networks are people, and links represent social relations (such as romantic relation).

COAUTHORSHIP NETWORKS

Coauthorship networks are two or more people working together to collaborate on a project. Wikipedia (an online encyclopedia) is a good example of a social media-based coauthorship network created by millions of authors from around the world(Biuk-Aghai 2006). A more explicit example of the coauthorship network is the ResearchGate platform: a social networking site for researchers to share articles, ask and respond to questions, and find collaborators. In these networks, nodes are, for example, researchers, and links represent the coauthorship relationship.

COCOMMENTER NETWORKS

Cocommenter networks are formed when two or more people comment on social media content (e.g., a Facebook status update, blog post, or YouTube video). A cocommenter network can, for example, be constructed from the comments posted by users in response to a video posted over YouTube or a Facebook fan page. In these networks, nodes represent users, and link represents the cocommenting relationship.

COLIKE

In a similar way, colike networks are formed when two or more people like the same social media content. Using NodeXL (a social network analysis tool), one can construct a network based on colikes (two or more people liking a similar content) over Facebook fan page. In such network, nodes will be Facebook users/fans and links will be the colikes relationship.

COOCCURRENCE NETWORK

Cooccurrence networks are formed when two more entities (e.g., keywords, people, ideas, and brands) cooccur over social media outlets. For example, one can construct a cooccurrence network of brand names (or people) to investigate how often certain brands (or people) cooccur over social media outlets. In such networks, nodes will be the brand names and the links will represent the cooccurrence relationships among the brands.

GEO COEXISTENCE NETWORK

Geo coexistence networks are formed when two more entities (e.g., people, devices, and addresses) coexist in a geographic location. In such a network nodes represents entities (e.g., people), and links among them represent coexistence.

HYPERLINK NETWORKS

In simple words, *hyperlink* is a mechanism to move among electronic documents (such as websites). Hyperlinks can be referred to as being either in-links (i.e., hyperlinks originating in other websites (Björneborn and Ingwersen 2004), thus bringing traffic/users to your website) or out-links (i.e., links originating in your website and going out (Bjorneborn 2001), thus sending traffic to other websites). Hyperlink also forms networks. Typically, in these network nodes are website, and links represent referral relationships (in the form of in-links or out-links). Hyperlink networks are discussed in a later chapter in detail.

TYPES OF NETWORKS

From a technical point of view, the above-mentioned networks can be classified in a variety of ways, including 1) based on existence, 2) based on direction of links, 3) based on mode, and 4) based on weights.

BASED ON EXISTENCE

Based on the way the networks exist online or are constructed, they can be classified as 1) implicit networks or 2) explicit networks.

Implicit Networks

Implicit networks do not exit by default (or are hidden) and need to be intentionally constructed with the help of dedicated tools and techniques. Examples of such networks include keyword cooccurrence networks, cocitation networks, cocommenter networks, hyperlink networks, etc. Constructing and studying implicit networks can provide valuable information and insights.

Explicit Networks

Explicit social media networks exist by default; in other words, they are explicitly designed for social media users to be part of. Most social media networks are explicit in nature. Examples of explicit social media networks include Facebook friendship network, Twitter follow-following networks, LinkedIn professional networks, YouTube subscribers' network, and bloggers' networks. In this chapter we will focus on explicit social media networks.

BASED ON DIRECTION

Based on the directions of links among the nodes, the networks can be classified as 1) directed networks, and 2) undirected networks.

Directed Networks

A network with directed links among nodes is called a directed network (Figure 6). Usually, a link with an arrow is drawn to show the direction of the relationship among the nodes. For example, the Twitter following-following network is a directed network where direction of the arrow shows who is following whom.

Undirected Network

In undirected networks, the links among the nodes do not have any direction. A Facebook friendship network is an example of undirected network.

BASED ON MODE

Based on the composition of nodes, networks can be classified as 1) one-mode network, 2) two-mode networks, and 3) multimode networks.

One-Mode Networks

A one-mode network is formed among a single set of nodes of the same nature (Figure 6). A Facebook friendship network is an example of a one-mode network where nodes (people) form network ties (friendships).

Two-Mode Networks

Two-mode networks (also known as bipartite networks) are networks with two sets of nodes of different classes (Latapy, Magnien et al. 2008). In these networks, network ties exist only between nodes belonging to different sets (Figure 6). For example, consider the two-mode network given in Figure 6, where one set of nodes (circles) could be social media users and other set of nodes (squares) could be participation in a series of events. Users are linked to the events they attended.

Multimode Network

A multimode network is also possible where multiple heterogeneous nodes are connected together. It can be considered as an amalgam of one and two-mode networks.

BASED ON WEIGHTS

Networks can also be classified based the weight assigned to the links among the nodes. Mainly there are two types of weighted networks: 1) weighted networks, and 2) unweighted networks.

Weighted Networks

In weighted networks, the links among nodes bear certain weights to indicate the strength of association among the nodes. The link (relationship) between, for example, two Facebook friends (nodes) will be thicker if they communicate more frequently (Figure 6). Weighted networks can provide rich information, but are difficult to construct.

UNWEIGHTED NETWORKS

In unweighted networks, links among nodes does not bear weights. The links only indicate the existence of a relationship and cannot provide clues about the strength of relationship (Figure 6). Un-weighted networks are easy to construct, but may conceal useful information.

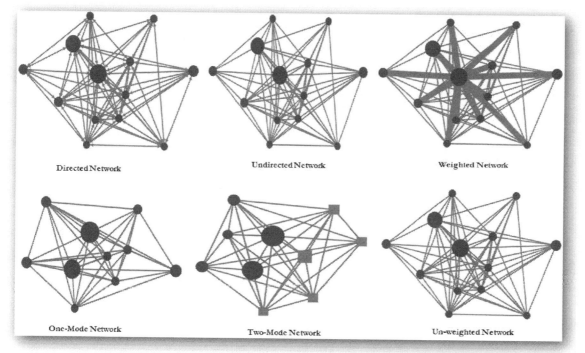

Figure 6. Types of social media networks

Keep in mind that the above-classified types are not mutually exclusive and can exist in a single network. For example, there may exist a directed weighted one-mode network. Or one could construct an undirected two-mode unweight network, and so forth.

COMMON NETWORK TERMINOLOGIES

Now, let's look at some common network terminologies or properties. Network properties can be divided into two categories 1) node-level properties, and 2) network-level properties.

NODE-LEVEL PROPERTIES

Node-level properties focus on one node and its position in the network. Some important node properties include degree centrality, betweenness centrality, eigenvector centrality, and structural holes.

Degree Centrality

Degree centrality of a node in a network measures the number of links a node has to other nodes (Hanneman and Riddle 2005). In a Facebook network, for example, this will measure the number friendship ties a user has. In a Twitter network, it will equate to the number of followers a user has. In a directed network, degree can be either in-degree or out-degree. In-degree is the number of incoming links a node in a network receives. For example, in a Twitter network, in-degree represents the number of followers a person has. Out-degree represents that number of out links a node sends. In a Twitter network, for example, the number of people a person follows represents out-degree of a person (node). In certain networks, such as a Twitter network, in-degree (number of followers a person has) is a more important measure of a node's influence than out-degree (number of people a person follows).

Betweenness Centrality

Betweenness centrality is related to the centrality (or position) of a node in a network. The nodes with high betweenness centrality have the ability to control or facilitate collaboration or flow of information due to their central position in the network (Liu, Bollen et al. 2005). In a Facebook friendship network, for example, the users who occupy the central position are better positioned to control the flow of social media content.

Eigenvector Centrality

Eigenvector centrality measures the importance of a node based on its connections with other important nodes in a network. It can provide an understanding of a node's networking ability relative to that of others (Marsden 2008).

Structural Holes

The idea of structural holes was first put forward by Burt (Burt 1992) who suggest that in a network exists when a certain node has an advantage or disadvantage of its location in a network (Hanneman and Riddle 2005). A node that is connected to users who are themselves not directly connected has the opportunity to mediate between them and profit from this mediation (Nooy, Mrvar et al. 2005). In a social media network, some users, because of their network position, may have an advantage or disadvantage in terms of opportunities to form and propagate information. New ideas and information mostly come from structure holes (or week ties) that exist in a network. A user with more week ties can receive novel ideas and information from remote network clusters.

NETWORK-LEVEL PROPERTIES

Network properties provide insight into the overall structure and health of a network. Important network-level properties include clustering coefficient, density, diameter, average degree, and components.

Clustering Coefficient

The clustering coefficient of a network is the degree to which nodes in a network tend to cluster or group together.

Density

The density of a network deals with a number of links in a network. Density can be calculated as the number of links present in a network divided by the number of all possible links between pairs of nodes in a network (for an undirected network, the number of all possible links can be calculated as $n(n-1)/2$; where n is the number of nodes in a network). A fully connected network, in which each node is connected to every other node, will have a density of 1.

Components

Components of a network are the isolated sub-networks that connect within, but are disconnected between, sub-networks (Hanneman and Riddle 2005). In a connected component, all nodes are connected and reachable, but there is no path between a node in the component and any node not in the component (Wasserman and Faust 1994). The main or largest component of a network is the component with the largest number of nodes.

Diameter

The diameter of a network is the largest of all the calculated shortest path between any pair of nodes in a network (Wasserman and Faust 1994), and it can provide an idea of how long it would take for some information/ideas/message to pass through the network.

Average Degree

The *average degree* centrality measures the average number of links among nodes in a network.

NETWORK ANALYTICS TOOLS

NodeXL: NodeXL (an add-in for Microsoft Excel) is the free tool for social network analysis and visualization. It can help you construct and analyze Facebook networks (based on colikes and cocomments), Twitter networks (followers, followings, and tweets), and YouTube networks (user network and comments), among others.

UCINET: UCINET is a social network analysis software application for windows operating system. It also includes Netdraw tool for network visualization. It can be downloaded and used for free for 90 days: https://sites.google.com/site/ucinetsoftware/home.

Pajek: Pajek is a software application for analyzing and visualizing large networks (http://mrvar.fdv.uni-lj.si/pajek/). Pajek runs on Microsoft Windows operating systems and is free for noncommercial use.

Netminer: Netminer (http://www.netminer.com/) is also a software application for large social network analysis and visualization. The application can used be for free for 28 days.

Flocker: Flocker (http://flocker.outliers.es/) is a Twitter real-time retweets and mentions networks analytics tool.

Reach: Reach is an online platform to map hashtag networks and identify the most influential accounts in the Twitter conversation: http://www.reach-social.com/.

Mentionmapp: This online tool is used to investigate Twitter mentions networks (http://mentionmapp.com/).

CASE STUDY: DO SOCIAL MEDIA NETWORKS REFLECT SOCIAL CULTURE?

BACKGROUND

Cultural values and norms form an integral part of a society in which "every person carries within him or herself patterns of thinking, feeling and potential acting which were learned throughout their lifetime" (Hofstede 1991)(p. 4). Research has shown that culture can have considerable influence on the use of technologies by people with different cultural backgrounds different cultures perceive technologies differently (Hofstede 1984; Hofstede 1991; Simon 2000). For example, a cross-cultural study of knowledge workers in the U.S. and Japan found that their cultural background played an important role in their predisposition toward and selection of technologies (e.g., telephone and fax) (Straub 1994). However, little is known about the effects of various cultural dimensions such as collectivism and individualism (Hofstede 1984) on social media use in the public sector. This raises the question of how differences in cultural norms (e.g., those of the U.S. and Korea) influence social media–use patterns and strategies in the public sector. This was the question a research team at Cyber Emotion Research Center at YeungNam University in South Korea was determined to investigate. The research team knew that answer could be found by mapping and analyzing social media networks formed by organizations from different cultures and were looking to leverage it. The hypothesis was that cultural difference may be reflected in the structures of social media networks formed among people from different societies.

WHAT THEY DID

Based on previous research on cultural difference, the team decided to investigate Twitter networks of Korean and U.S ministries. Korea is a hierarchical, collectivistic, and feminine society that avoids uncertainty and emphasizes collectivism, whereas the U.S. is a nonhierarchical, individualistic, and masculine society that accepts uncertainty and emphasizes individualism (Hofstede 1984; Hofstede 1991). The researchers were of the opinion that a cross-cultural comparison of social media networks between Korean and U.S governments may provide a better understanding of the diverse patterns of social media use in the public sector.

To this end, the research team compiled a list of Twitter accounts used by the 40 Korean and 32 U.S. government agencies. Using the accounts, the data on Twitter following-followers network was collected. The data was collected by using an in-house software program designed based on the API provided by Twitter.com. The program can be used to submit queries to Twitter.com and process results. Once the network data was harvested, NodeXL was used to construct and visualize the networks. In addition, with the help of a research assistant, some follow-up telephone interviews were conducted with the manager in charge of the Twitter accounts in selected ministries. The purpose of the interviews was to get a first-hand account of the Twitter communication strategies in the ministries that had dedicated social media staff.

RESULTS

The results were surprising and showed clear structural differences between the two Twitter networks. Figure 7 shows these differences. For example, Korean ministries were well connected in a dense network of follower-following relationships, whereas U.S. government departments tended to be loosely connected. In terms of network density, the Korean network (density = 0.86) was substantially denser than the U.S. network (density = 0.26). This density is a simple but useful measure of group cohesiveness. The Korean network had 1,348 (86%) ties, whereas the U.S. network had only 255 (26%). The clustering coefficient (i.e., the degree to which nodes in a network tend to cluster together) was higher for the Korean network (0.86) than for the U.S. network (0.50), indicating that the Korean network was more likely to form "cliques." In other words, Korean ministries tended to be locally embedded in dense neighborhoods (clusters). This was supported by the average degree (the average number of other government agencies followed by a government agency), which was much higher for Korean accounts (33) than for U.S. accounts (7.9). This indicates that, unlike U.S. government departments, almost all Korean ministries followed all other ministries.

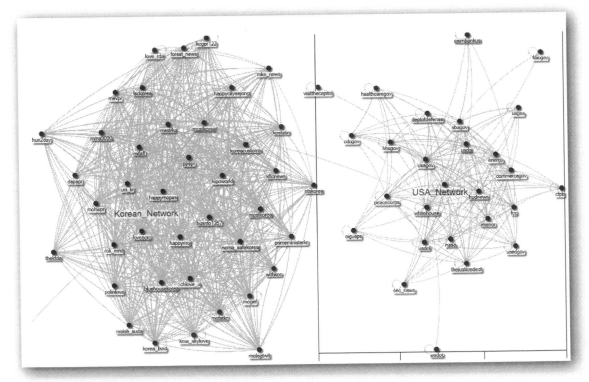

Figure 7. Follow-following Twitter network diagram of Korean and US public sector organizations

WHAT WE LEARN FROM THE CASE STUDY

The case study highlights the usefulness of social media network and how it can be used to answer interesting real world research questions. The research provided some new insights into the effects of cultural values and social norms (e.g., collectivism vs. individualism) on the pattern of Twitter networks in the public sector. For example, Korea is a collectivistic society, whereas the U.S. is an individualistic one (Hofstede 1984). In this regard, the result indicating a dense Twitter network of Korean ministries may reflect the country's collective norms in the online environment. Unlike organizations from individualistic cultures such as the U.S., who were loosely connected and tended to be interested more in engaging in individual communication (e.g., tweets) than in forming dense networks to pursue collective agendas.

Source: the case study is compiled from the study by Khan et al (2014). Complete research can be accessed from: Khan, G. F. Young, H., & Park, H. W. (2014). Social Media Communication strategies of Governments: A comparison of the USA and S. Korean governments, Asian Journal of Communication (SSCI), Vol. 24, No. 1, 2014, pp. 60–78.

TUTURIAL: ANALYZING SOCIAL MEDIA NETWORKS WITH NodeXL

NodeXL is an easy and powerful tool for extracting, analyzing and visualizing social media networks. It is an add-in or template for Microsoft Excel and compatible with Excel 2007, Excel 2010, and Excel 2013. It can help you construct and analyze Facebook networks (based on colikes and cocomments), Twitter networks (followers, followings, and tweets network), and YouTube networks (user network and comments), among others. In this tutorial, we will cover the most important features of NodeXL. A detailed tutorial on NodeXL can be found on http://nodexl.codeplex.com/. You can also download an up-to-date NodeXL tutorial with several screenshots from the book companion site: http://7layersanalytics.com/.

INSTALLING AND RUNNING NodeXL

Step 1: Go to the http://nodexl.codeplex.com/ and download the latest version of the NodeXL template, then run it.

Step 2: Click "accept" when you are offered the license agreement.

Step 3: If you are asked to accept the "Microsoft Visual Studio 2010 Tools for Office Runtime (x86 and x64)," click the "Accept" button.

Step 4: If you are asked to reboot, click "Yes" to reboot your computer.

Step 5: When you are asked "Are you sure you want to install this customization?" click the "Install" button.

Step 6: To open NodeXL after installation, in the Windows Start menu or Start screen, search for "NodeXL," then click "NodeXL Excel Template" in the search results.

After it is opened, you will notice that NodeXL has its own menu ribbon available at the top right (Screenshot 6), and that the first Excel worksheet is called Edges (i.e., nodes). Other default four main worksheets are "Vertices" (i.e., links), "Groups," "Group Vertices," and "Overall Metrics." The Groups worksheet groups the nodes by common attributes. NodeXL analyzes their connectedness and automatically groups them into clusters. The Overall Metrics worksheet shows the overall network measures, for example, density, degree, clustering coefficient, betweenness centrality, etc.

Screenshot 6. NodeXL template

UNDERSTANDING NODEXL WORKFLOW

Figure 8 shows the work flow of NodeXL, which consists mainly of four steps: 1) importing data, 2) cleaning data, 3) calculating network analysis, and 4) visualizing the network. We will go through each of the stages in detail.

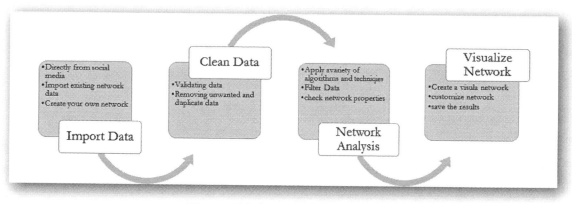

Figure 8. NodeXL work flow stages

Stage 1: Importing Network Data

The first step in analyzing networks with NodeXL is to import the network data. In NodeXL, network data can be imported from a variety of sources and formats, including Pajek files, UCINET[2], other spreadsheets, and comma separated value (CSV) files, and directly from social media sites. You can also start creating your own network by manually typing a list of the edges in the network into the NodeXL sheet. With NodeXL social imports/plug-ins, data from a variety of social networks can be directly imported, including Facebook, Twitter, YouTube, Flickr, e-mail, Exchange, wikis, and surveys. Social importers are regularly updated, and new social importers are made available on the NodeXL website. To add new social importers, use the following steps.

Importing Third-party Data Importers

Step 1: Download the installation zip file from the NodeXL social importer website: http://socialnetimporter.codeplex.com/

Step 2: Unzip it and save it on your desktop (or any other location). After unzipping it, you will find the following four items:

FacebookAPI.DLL
FacebookAPI.pdb
SocialNetImporter.DLL
SocialNetImporter.pdb

---

2 Pajek and UNINET are social network analysis tools with their own network data formats and mechanisms.

Step 3: Now open the NodeXL template and then go to Import>Import Options>Browse. Locate and select the unzipped files you have just downloaded and then click "OK."

Step 4: Close and restart NodeXL. You should now see the "Facebook Import" option in the NodeXL> Import menu.

Note that other data importers (e.g., e-mail, wiki, and VOSON) can be accessed and installed in a similar fashion by going to NodeXL>Data>Import menu>Get third-party Graph Data Importers.

In this tutorial, we will import data directly from a Facebook network.

Importing a Social Media Network Directly

Step 1: Open the NodeXL template and then click on File→Import. Note that there are a variety of options to import data from. For this exercise, we'll use a Facebook fan page network.

Step 2: Then click on "Import from Facebook Fan Page Networks."

Step 3: Next, you will be provided with the "Import from Facebook Fan Page Networks" dialogue box (Screenshot 7). In order to import the network, NodeXL should be authorized. Click on the "Log in" button available at the bottom of the dialogue box. Provide your Facebook username and password in the Facebook login window, then click "Log In."

Step 4: Once you are connected to Facebook, you will be able to provide your Facebook fan page name or ID in specified field. The ID or name of the fan page can be found in the fan page URL.

In this tutorial, we will extract data from the Centre for Social Technologies Facebook fan page. Select all the other desired options provided in the "Import from Facebook Fan Page Networks" dialogue box, such as network nodes (e.g., users will become nodes in the network), type of network relations (e.g., likes and comment will become links among the nodes), and edge creation options. You may also change the limit on the number of posts to include or specify a particular date for data extractions. Depending on the size of the activity on the fan page, choosing several options may cause it to take a long time to extract the data. Once you are ready, click the "Download" button to extract the network.

Screenshot 7. Import from Facebook fan page window

Stage 2: Cleaning the Network Data

After the network data is downloaded, sift through the NodeXL worksheets and verify and clean the data if necessary. If the data looks good, proceed to the analysis stage.

Stage 3: Network Analysis

Step 1: Calculate the network properties by clicking on the "Graph Metrics" option available at the top to the NodeXL window.

Step 2: In the "Graph Metrics" window, select all the network measures of interest (e.g., overall graph metrics, degree, betweenness centrality, clustering coefficient, etc.) and then click on the "Calculate Metrics" button.

The network measure will be calculated and added to the NodeXL worksheets. You can explore, for example, the overall network measures in the "Overall Metrics" worksheet of the NodeXL. You can see that the network has 293 nodes and 1,216 edges (or links among the nodes). From the network density and diameter, it is clear the network is very sparse.

Step 4: Next, click on the "Show Graph" button to visualize the network.

Step 6: The constructed network will be displayed. However, the network is basic and does not carry much information (Screenshot 8).

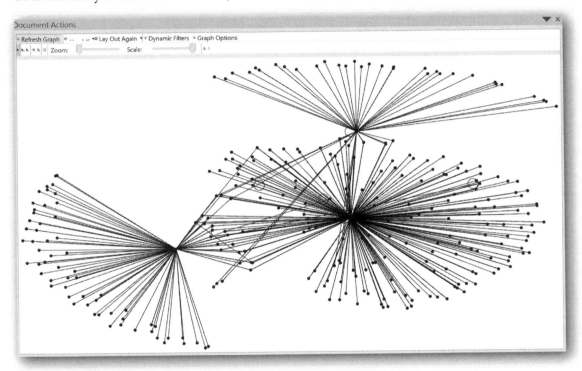

Screenshot 8. Facebook fan page network

Step 7: To make the network more constructive or informative, click on the "Autofill Columns" button available at the top of the NodeXL window.

Step 8: With the "Autofill Columns" functionality, you can alter the node and edge appearance (e.g., size, shape, color, opacity, or label) according to the network properties, such as degree centrality, betweenness centrality, clustering coefficient, and page rank. For example, node size can present importance (betweenness centrality), edge size can represent strength of relationships among the nodes, and color of a node can be coded as gender.

Step 9: Click on the "Autofill Columns" and resize the vertices (fans) according to their in-degree centrality (so that the size of the node will represent importance in terms of the number connections a person has) (Screenshot 9). Also, set "Vertex Shape" to gender and color (in our dataset, gender is coded as 1=male, and 2=female). To do so, click on the "Options" arrow and set 1= Disk and 2= Solid Squire.

Screenshot 9. "Autofill Columns" window for vertices

Next, select the "Edge" tab, and set the width of the edge according to the number of comments/likes, so that the width of the link represents the strength of the relationships among the nodes in terms of the number of comments/likes received. Set "Edge Label" to "Edge Type" to display the type of relationship among the nodes, such as Liker, Commenter, Post Author, Co-Liker, etc. Next, click the "Autofill" button to redraw the network.

Now the network conveys more useful insights (Screenshot 10). It is clear that there are three important male fans (circle nodes with bigger size) in the network that drive most of the network activity, and that liking accounts for the majority of the network activity.

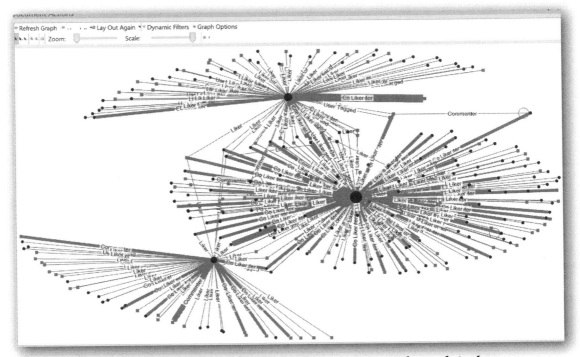

Screenshot 10. Facebook fan network: node size proportional to node in-degree and node color and shape mapped to the Gender. Circle nodes are male and squares are female fans. Links represents type of relations (Liker, Commenters, and Users Tagged, etc.) and width of the links represents its strength.

FURTHER ADJUSTMENTS

Several useful adjustments can be performed to the network with the NodeXL template; below, we briefly discuss some of important options.

Adjust Layout: with the help of "Adjust Layout," you can adjust the layout of the network (i.e., where each node in the network will be located) using a variety of different algorithms available at the "Adjust Layout" dropdown list. These include a force-directed Fruchterman-Reingold layout algorithm for automatically grouping tightly connected nodes together, as well as circles, grids, and spirals.

Apply Dynamic Filters: Dynamic filters trim parts of the network and then recalculate network metrics and layout based on the remaining nodes and edges. With dynamic filters, edges and nodes can be selectively hidden or shown, depending on the attributes of the network. For example, the in-degree filter will hide less important nodes.

Graph Options: Graph options allow further customization of the network layout, such as changing edge color, arrow size, and curvature. An updated network is shown (in the Screenshot 11) after the application of some these options.

SAVING THE NETWORK

Saving the diagram: To save the network diagram to your computer, right-click on the network diagram and then click on "Save Image of File→Save Image."

Saving the network data: The network data can be saved into its native NodeXL format for future use ("File→Save"), or it can exported into a different format to be used in different network analysis tools (such as UCINET and Pajek files). The "Export" menu is available at the top left corner of the NodeXL window (below "Import").

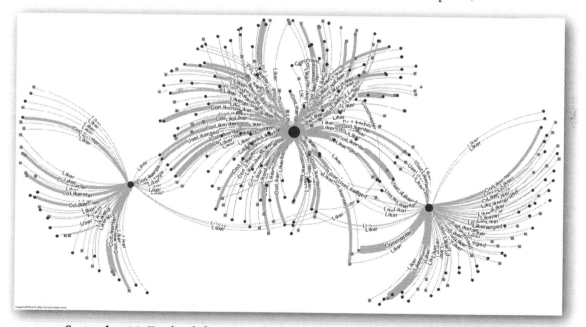

Screenshot 11. Facebook fan network after application of graph options: node size proportional to node in-degree and node color and shape mapped to gender. Circle nodes are male fans and square nodes are female fans. Links represents type of relationships (likers, commenters, users tagged, etc.) and width of the links represent their strength.

Review Questions

1. What is a network?
2. What is the purpose of network analytics?
3. Briefly differentiate among social networks, social network sites, social networking, and social network analysis.
4. Briefly explain the different types of social media networks.
5. What is the difference between explicit and implicit networks?
6. What is the difference between one-mode, two-mode, and multimode networks?
7. Differentiate between weighted and unweighted networks.
8. Briefly define important node level properties, such as degree, betweenness, eigenvector centralities, and structural holes.
9. Briefly explain important network-level properties, such as clustering coefficient, density, diameter, average degree, and components.

CHAPTER 5

SOCIAL MEDIA ACTIONS ANALYTICS

A CTIONS ARE the cash cow of social media. It is what the users do on social media that matters most to social media marketers. Typical actions performed by social media users include likes, dislikes, shares, views, clicks, tags, mentions, recommendations, and endorsements. Actions are way to express symbolic reactions to social media content. Symbolic actions are an easy and fast way to express feelings, unlike written reaction in the form of textual comments. Actions are not just symbolic reactions; they carry emotions and behaviors that can be harnessed. More importantly, social media actions are social expressions; that is, a user who performs an action (e.g., liking certain content) is visible to (or shared with) other social media users, in particular with their friends. This shareable nature of social media actions makes it very attractive to social media marketers and businesses. Take as an example Moviefone (an American-based movie listing and information service company), which enabled logins with Facebook and Twitter credentials. Enabling such login services not only allow users to use the Moviefone service conveniently, but also let them connect with their social media friends and share content over the Moviefone site. Enabling social logins led to a 300 percent increase in site traffic, a 40,000 to 250,000 increase in referrals per month, and a 40 percent increase in click-through rate (Petersen 2012).

WHAT IS ACTIONS ANALYTICS?

Social media actions analytics deals with extraction, analysis, and interpretation of the insights contained in the actions performed by social media users. Social media actions are of great value to social media marketers because of their role in increasing revenue, brand value, and loyalty. Organizations can employ actions analytics to measure popularity and influence of a product, service, or idea over social media. For example, a brand marketer might be interested to know how popular their new product is among social media users. Analyzing your Facebook likes and Twitter mentions, for example, may provide an answer to your questions.

COMMON SOCIAL MEDIA ACTIONS

Below, we briefly discuss some of the most prevalent social media actions. All these actions are performed by social media users and can become your social media metrics. Metrics, in simple words, are anything you want to measure. Social media users can come in many forms, including followers, fans, and subscribers.

LIKE

Like or "Like" buttons or like options are a feature of social media sites (e.g., social networks, blogs, and websites) that allow users to express their feelings of liking certain products, services, people, ideas, information, places, or content. They are actions performed by social media users to express symbolic positive reaction to social media content. Facebook's "Like" button enables users to easily express their feelings and give your product or service a virtual thumbs up. Incorporating a "Like" button in social media platforms and websites is becoming a norm. Social media platforms display accumulated likes received by content over time. Facebook's "Like" button is the most famous one. Google+ social networking platform uses a "+1" symbol to express liking. Companies use Google+ and Facebook fan pages to receive likes from customers, but the "Like" button can also be incorporated into a company website or blog. The "Like" button can be easily incorporated into a website as follows:

1. Visit Facebook's developers' page: https://developers.facebook.com/docs/plugins/like-button
2. Customize and generate a code.
3. Paste the code into your website after the <body> tag.

DISLIKE

"Dislike" buttons are included in some social media platforms (e.g., YouTube) and allow users to express their negative feelings of disliking certain content (e.g., products, services, people, ideas, information, or places) posted over social media. Similar to the "Like" feature, it is visible to others and accumulated over time. The "Dislike" button is not as prevalent as the "Like" button.

SHARE

Share or "Share" button or sharing is a feature that allows social media users to distribute the content posted over social media to other users. For example, the Facebook "Share" button lets users add a personal message and customize who they share the content with. The WordPress (a blogging platform) "Share" button, for example, allows users to share their blog content across a range of social media platforms. Companies incorporate share buttons into website to boost their website traffic by channeling visitors from social media sites.

VISITORS, VISITS, REVISITS

A visitor is a person who visits your website or blog. A single visitor may visit a page or content one or more times (revisits). Visits are also known as sessions. Other related concepts are:

Unique visitor—A person who arrives at your page first time.

Average bounce rate—the percentage of visitors who visit a website and leave the site quickly without viewing other pages.

Session duration—The average duration of a visit or session.

VIEW

Views are the number of times social media content (a post, video, graphic, etc.) is viewed by users. A slightly different but related concept is page views, which is each time a visitor views a page on your company website or blog.

CLICKS

Clicks are the actions performed by users by pressing or clicking on the hyperlinked content of your website or blog. Through clicks, users navigate the web. Click data can be harvested for business intelligence purposes, such as, to reduce bounce rate and improve website traffic. A technique called *clickstream analysis* is used by business managers for a variety of business intelligence purposes, including website activity, website design analysis, path optimization, market research, and finding ways to improve visitor experience on the website. The clickstream is the semistructured data trail/log (such as date and time stamp, IP address, and the URLs of the pages visited) a user leaves while visiting a website.

Tagging

Tagging is the act of assigning or linking extra pieces of information to social media content (such as photographs and bookmarks) for identification, classification, and search purposes. Tagging lets user classify social media content the way they see it. Tagging may take a variety of forms. For example, bloggers can attach descriptive keywords (tags) to their posts to facilitate classification and searching of content, and Facebook users can add tags to anything they post on their status, including photos and comments. Social bookmarking services (such as del.icio.us) let users organize their bookmarks flexibly by adding descriptive tags. This practice of collaborative tagging is commonly known as *folksonomy*—a term coined by Thomas Vander Wal (Wal 2005). These days, almost all prominent companies (e.g., Facebook and Flickr) provide tagging services to their users. Because the contents are tagged with useful keywords, social tagging expedites the process of searching and finding relevant content.

Mentions

Mentions or social mentions are the occurrence of a person, place, or thing over social media by name. For example, a brand name maybe mentioned in a Facebook comment, blog post, YouTube video, or tweet. Mentions are important and can indicate popularity of person, place, or thing. For example, a social marketer may be able to gauge the popularity of a product/service/campaign by mining Twitter mentions data. A Twitter mention is the inclusion of a "@username" in a tweet.

Hovering

Hovering is the act of moving a cursor over social media content. Capturing users' cursor movement data can help you understand user behavior on a social media site. Cursor movement/hovering over an ad, for example, can be considered as a proxy for attention. Most people who view an ad do not necessary click on it, thus if we are relying on clicks analytics only, we may lose a vital piece of information (i.e., attention). Studies have even suggested a strong correlation between hover time and purchases. Traditionally, hovering data has been used in website design and for improvement of user experience.

CHECK-IN

Check-in is a social media feature that allows users to announce and share their arrival at a location, such as a hotel, airport, city, or store. Many social media services, including Facebook and Google+, provide check-in features. The location of the user is determined using GPS (global positioning system) technology. Check-in data can, for example, be mined to offer location-based services/products.

PINNING

Pinning is an action performed by social media users to pin and share interesting content (such as ideas, products, services, and information) using a virtual pin-board platform. Some famous pinning platforms include Pinterest, Tumblr, StumbleUpon, or Digg. Business can use these virtual pin boards to share information and connect with and inspire their customers. Four Seasons Hotels and Resorts, for example, use Pinterest to curate travel, food, and luxury lifestyle content to inspire customers.

EMBEDS

Embedding is the act of incorporating social media content (e.g., a link, video, or presentation) into a website or blog. An embed feature lets users embed interesting content into their personal social media outlets.

ENDORSEMENT

Endorsement is a features of social media that lets people endorse and approve other people, products, and services. For example, LinkedIn lets user endorse the skills and qualifications of other people in their network.

UPLOADING AND DOWNLOADING

In simple words, uploading is the act of adding new content (e.g., texts, photos, and videos) to a social media platform. The opposite of uploading is downloading; that is, the act of receiving data from a social media platform. All most all social media content is created and uploaded by users, which is better known as user-generated content. For some companies, uploading and downloading is the single most important action to measure. For Instagram and Flickr, which are both photo-sharing platforms, the number of photos uploaded daily matters more than anything else.

Actions Analytics Tools

Currently, there is no single platform that can capture all the actions discussed in this chapter. Certain platforms can be employed to measure social media actions across platforms. Below we list some popular actions analytics tools.

Hootsuite: Hootsuite is an easy-to-use online platform that enables you to manage your social media presence across the most popular social networks. Hootsuite offers different plans depending on your business needs and budget: free, pro, or enterprise. In this tutorial, we will employ the free version, which supports up to five social media profiles and has limited analytics information.

SocialMediaMineR: SocialMediaMineR is a social media analytics tool that takes one or multiple URLs and returns the information about the popularity and reach of the URL(s) on social media, including the number of shares, likes, tweets, pins, and hits on Facebook, Twitter, Pinterest, StumbleUpon, LinkedIn, and Reddit. The tool can accessed from here: http://cran.r-project.org/web/packages/SocialMediaMineR/index.html

Lithium: Lithium (http://www.lithium.com/) is social media management tool that provides a variety of products and services, including social media analytics, marking, crowd-sourcing, and social media marketing.

Google Analytics: Google Analytics (http://www.google.com/analytics/) is an analytical tool offered by Google to track and analyze website traffic. It can also be used to for blogs and wiki analytics.

Facebook Insights: Facebook Insights (https://www.facebook.com/insights/) helps Facebook page owners understand and analyze trends within user growth and demographics.

Klout: Klout (https://klout.com/) measures your influence across a range of social media channels based on how many people interact with your posts. Your Klout score measures your influence on a scale from one to one hundred.

Topsy: Topsy (http://topsy.com/) is similar to Icerocket and Social Mention, with its main focus around social media, especially multimedia sites and blogs.

Tweetreach: This tool helps you measure the number of impressions and reach of hashtags. The tool can be accessed here: https://tweetreach.com

Kred: Kred helps you measure the influence of a Twitter account: www.kred.com

Hashtagify: This tool measures the influence of hashtags: http://hashtagify.me

Twtrland: Twtrland is a social intelligence research tool (http://twtrland.com/) for analyzing and visualizes your social footprints.

Tweetstats: using your Twitter user name, Tweetstats graphs Twitter stats including tweets per hour, tweets per month, tweet timelines, and reply statistics (http://www.tweetstats.com).

CASE STUDY: COVER-MORE GROUP

VISUALIZING THE ROI OF SOCIAL

The heart of travel insurance provider Cover-More's social efforts is its Social Media Command Center, a unique way to provide customer feedback and performance metrics in an easy-to-understand visual display. Here's how the social media team took control of the unwieldy task of presenting analytics and came out looking like stars.

COVER-MORE GROUP

Cover-More Group is an Australian-owned global travel insurance and assistance group with offices in Australia, the United Kingdom, China, India, New Zealand, and Malaysia. Each year, Cover-More provides insurance policies for over 1.6 million travelers, manages more than 70,000 insurance claims, and helps more than 42,000 customers with emergency assistance.

WHAT THEY DID

Cover-More had three main objectives in building a Social Media Command Center:

- To prove the ROI on social media efforts to stakeholders.
- To provide a snapshot of Cover-More's social media presence to the board of directors.
- To give a real-time feel to reporting and automate the process.

At the board level, Cover-More needed to be able to show a snapshot of how the company's social strategy was progressing, particularly in comparison with competitors. They were also keen to show executives how social media could benefit the business and not just be seen as a risk. However, the social media and eCommerce teams wanted to know how their activities were tracking on a day-to-day basis. Reconciling the reporting needs of executives and practitioners was proving difficult.

Once a month, Lynton Manuel, Cover-More's Social Media Manager, would populate a spreadsheet with data from each of the company's social network profiles, in an attempt to put the various channels and results in context with one another. The process was inefficient and labor-intensive: dedicating half a day each month to compile a "pseudo dashboard" became the norm. Manuel presented an overview of status, successes, and challenges to the Board of Directors monthly, but the Board was most interested in a visual snapshot. Realizing that executives—or anyone within the business that doesn't have knowledge of different platforms—needed a more simplified, visually attractive way to interact with the data, the social media team decided that Hootsuite's Social Media Command Center was the solution.

HOW THEY DID IT

The Cover-More social media team needed to bring social media intelligence into the company's nerve center via a large display in order to inform and impress viewers. So, with the help of the IT department, they set up a 60-inch television in a prominent location where employees, executives, and potential clients could see it. The team decided on what they wanted to display and set up the Command Center using a number of adjustable Hootsuite widgets via a simple drag-and-drop process. From there, it was just a matter of adjusting the Hootsuite Analytics, Streams, and Monitoring features to customize the display. The team picked specific widgets like Mentions, Sentiment, Exposure, and Sharing, making it quick and easy to choose what information meant the most to them, to the executives, and to prospective and current clients.

By integrating the Social Media Command Center, the social media team was able to:

Show the positive impact of the social media team's efforts to executives. After the Command Center went live, a senior executive saw the most recent tweets and remarked, "I didn't know we had people saying thanks on Twitter. This looks fantastic."

Increase employee engagement and morale. Employees were able to quickly understand the real-time data, which demonstrated the company's leadership in the social media sphere. ‹

Customize the Command Center screen for maximum brand visibility. The company's graphic designer created a custom background image and incorporated style elements to make sure the Command Center was visually appealing and on-brand.

THE RESULTS

Within the first few weeks of operation, the Social Media Command Center had not only impressed the executives and colleagues at CoverMore, but external clients as well. A visiting prospective client saw the display and, recognizing his own company name in the feed, was impressed enough with the Cover-More's digital savvy that he signed up with the company. With relatively little set-up time and effort, the social media team had improved its own efficiency (no more monthly spreadsheet updates) and had provided specific examples of how their efforts were directly impacting the business.

Source: Hootsuite, https://hootsuite.com/resources/case-study/transforming-data-into-action-cover-more-group

TUTORIAL: ANALYZING SOCIAL MEDIA ACTIONS WITH HOOTSUITE

The tutorial assumes that you already have your social media profiles configured (such as a Twitter account and Facebook fan page). Below are the step-by-step guidelines to configure and use Hootsuite. You can also download an up-to-date Hootsuite tutorial with several screenshots from the book companion site: http://7layersanalytics.com/.

Step 1: To start using the free version, go to http://signup.hootsuite.com/plans-cc/ and click on the "Get Started Now" button available under the free version.

Step 2: Next, provide your e-mail address and name, choose a strong password, and then click on the "Create Account" button.

Step 3: Click on the "Twitter" button available under the "Connect Your Social Network" section. Note that you can choose several social media accounts to manage using Hootsuite. For now, we will only configure Twitter and Facebook.

Step 4: A popup window will open asking you to authorize Hootsuite to access your Twitter account. Here, provide your Twitter username (or e-mail) and password and then click on the "Authorize App" button.

Step 5: After authorization, your Twitter account will appear in the added accounts. Next, click the "Continue" button. Note that you can add multiple accounts.

Step 6: Click on the "Get Started" button to complete the three simple steps (i.e., adding streams, creating a tab, and scheduling a message) suggested by Hootsuite.

Adding Streams

Step 7: To monitor conversations and actions over Twitter, you need to add streams (Screenshot 12). To do so, click on all the streams you are interested in monitoring (e.g., tweets, mentions, and retweets).

Screenshot 12. Hootsuite Dashboard

Step 8: Streams will start appearing on your Hootsuite.

Creating a tab

Step 9: Tabs are used to group stream-based interests or similarities. To add a tab, click on the **+** icon.

Step 10: Name the new tab (e.g., Followers) and click "Next."

Scheduling a Message

Step 11: With Hootsuite you can post messages to several social media platforms (e.g., Twitter and Facebook) either instantly or for later. To write a message, click to select the social profile(s) that will post your message (in this case Twitter). Click "Compose Message," and then type message. After writing the message, either click the "Send Now" button or the "Calendar" icon to schedule it for later. This step will complete the initial configuration of Hootsuite.

ANALYTICS WITH HOOTSUITE

Hootsuite provides two ways to generate analytics reports: 1) using premade templates, and 2) creating custom-made analytics reports. Note that the free version has limited analytics abilities, and you will be able to use only a limited number of templates.

To use Hootsuite's premade templates, go through the following steps:

Step 1: Click the bar graph (Analytics) icon on the left-aligned launch menu.

Step 2: You can choose from several report templates. For example, click on the "Twitter Profile Overview" template.

Step 3: Click on the "Create Report" button. Note that you can have multiple social media accounts configured. You may choose them from the dropdown list.

Step 4: Next, the report will be generated.

Step 5: A report can be printed, saved as a PDF or CSV, shared with others, etc., by using the tool bar available at the top right corner of the report.

Creating Custom Reports

Step 1: Click the bar graph (Analytics) icon on the left-aligned launch menu.

Step 2: Click "Build Custom Report."

Step 3: Click "Custom Report."

Step 4: This will bring you to the custom report page.

Step 5: Click **"Upload Image"** to upload your logo or an image to brand the report. This is done by locating the image file on your computer and clicking "Open." You can also edit the details of your organization and type of header in the report.

Step 6: Under "Details" in the top left corner, type the title of your report and a brief description. And under "E-mail and Scheduling," click the dropdown menu and select the frequency of distribution.

Tip: You can also have this report e-mailed to the members sharing this report by clicking on the box, making a check.

Step 7: Next, click on "Add Report Modules" and then click to select the module, adding it to your report. Modules with ENT and PRO are only available to enterprise users.

Note: Modules added to your report can be removed by clicking "Remove" in the top right corner of the module on the report.

Step 8: Complete the information requested by that module to achieve the best results. This may involve typing a title and/or keywords, selecting a social network profile, and so forth, and then clicking "Done."

Step 9: Click on the "Create Report" button available at the top right of the page. Alternatively, you can click "Save as Draft."

Monitoring and Analyzing Facebook Data with Hootsuite

Step 1: First, you need to add a new tab for the Facebook network. To do so, click the home (streams) icon on the left-aligned launch menu, and then click on the + icon.

Step 2: Name the new tab (e.g., Facebook).

Step 3: Click on the "Add Social Network" button.

Step 4: Select Facebook from the list, and click on the "Connect with Facebook" button.

Step 5: Type your Facebook e-mail (or mobile phone number) and password, and then click "Log In."

Step 6: Next, read Hootsuite's access to your Facebook account message; click to read "App Terms and Privacy Policy" in the bottom left corner, and then click "OK."

Step 7: Read posting permission note, click to select who can see the content you post to Facebook from Hootsuite, and then click "Okay."

Note: Clicking "Skip" will prevent you from being able to post to Facebook from Hootsuite.

Step 8: Read the page permission note, and then click "Okay."

Note: Clicking "Skip" will prevent you from being able to manage your Facebook pages from Hootsuite.

Step 9: Click to select the timeline, pages, and groups to import. A check mark indicates that the content will be imported; a plus icon indicates the content will not be imported. When done, click "Finished Importing."

Adding a Facebook Stream

Now that Facebook is added to Hootsuite, it is time to add streams to measure.

Step 1: Click the home (streams) icon on the left-aligned launch menu, then click the tab hosting your Facebook content.

Step 2: Next, click "Add Stream."

Step 3: Select Facebook and then select a profile that will stream content (in this case, we added a fan page) (Screenshot 13).

Add Stream   ✕

	Stream Search
▣ Twitter	**Select a profile:**
▣ Facebook	🐾 Center for Social Technol... ⌄
▣ Google+	**Click a stream to add to the current tab:**
▣ LinkedIn	Timeline ✚
ⓦ WordPress	Events ✚
▣ Apps	Scheduled ✚
	Messages ✚
	Unpublished ✚
	Posts to page ✚
	My Posts ✚
	Activity ✚

Screenshot 13. Adding a stream in Hotsuite

Step 4: Click the **+** button across from the stream to add. This process can be repeated for multiple Facebook streams.

Similar steps can be repeated for configuring Twitter, Google+, Wordpress, and LinkedIn streams for analytical purposes.

Review Questions

1. Define social media actions analytics.
2. Briefly list and define different actions performed by social media users.
3. Why it important to measure actions performed by social media users?

CHAPTER 6

MOBILE ANALYTICS

MOBILE APPLICATIONS are becoming an integral part of our lives. Applications (or apps) are special-purpose software developed to perform certain tasks on the go. Each app has a specific function and runs on specific mobile devices, such as smartphones, tablet computers, and smart watches. Mobile devices use a special type of operating system called a mobile operating system (or mobile OS). Popular mobile OSes are Android (from Google), iOS (from Apple computers), Windows Phone (from Microsoft), and BlackBerry 10 (From BlackBerry). Specific apps are developed for each mobile OS. Most apps (but not all) are made available online for download through application distributors (or app stores), such as the Apple Store, Google Play, and the Amazon apps store. According http://www.statista.com/, as of July 2014, there were 2.5 million apps available for download in the Apple Store and Google Play alone. App stores also provide opportunities to users to comment on and rate apps.

What Is Mobile Analytics?

Generally, mobile analytics may refer to two things, 1) mobile web analytics and 2) apps analytics.

Mobile Web Analytics

Mobile web analytics is mostly focused on characteristics, actions, and behaviors of mobile website visitors; that is, the visitors to the mobile version of your company's website. It is very similar to the conventional website analytics in scope and methodology. Companies collect and analyze a variety of mobile user data, including views, clicks, demographic information, and device-specific data (e.g., the type of mobile device used to access the website).

Apps Analytics

Apps analytics, however, deal with understanding and analyzing mobile application users' characteristics, actions, and behaviors. The subject of this chapter is apps analytics. These days all companies, big or small, are using mobile apps to drive sales, improve brand affinity, and make purchases possible with a few swipes. Korean Air apps, for example, let customer search and book flights with swipes on their smartphones. To make the most out of mobile apps, companies also need to have a deep understanding their customers and their characteristics. In this book, we focus on apps analytics.

Purpose of Apps Analytics

The main purpose of apps analytics is to measure and analyze user behavior; improve user experiences; and drive revenue, engagements, and loyalty. Some sample questions that can be answered with app analytics are provided below.

- ✓ Who are my users?
- ✓ Which countries are they from?
- ✓ What actions they are taking?
- ✓ How do my customers navigate in the app?
- ✓ What are my in-app payments and revenue?
- ✓ How long do they stay on my app?
- ✓ Which operator, operation system, and devices they use?
- ✓ What item is purchased the most?
- ✓ Which countries were top performers in terms of in-app purchases?
- ✓ Which application version leads to more sales?
- ✓ How long do my users stay inside my application?
- ✓ How often do my users open my app?
- ✓ How many users started a specific number of sessions?
- ✓ How do my applications versions compare to one another?

The types of question you can answer also depend on the apps analytics platform you use.

Types of Apps

Apps can be classified mainly in two ways: 1) from the perspective of development and deployment and 2) from the perspective of objectives.

FROM THE PERSPECTIVE OF DEVELOPMENT

The way mobile apps are developed and deployed, they can be classified into three types: 1) native apps, 2) web-based apps, and 3) hybrid apps (Korf and Oksman 2014). Let's look at each of them briefly.

Native Apps

Native apps are specifically created for and installed on mobile devices. Native apps are device specific; that is, they are created to work on a particular mobile device. For example, apps for Android-based mobile devices are created in Java programming language, and iOS apps are created in objective C and Cocoa programming (a programming language native to Apple devices). If a business, for example, wants to create an app that can run both on Android and iOS, they may need to develop two separate versions. Native apps are made available for download in apps stores (such as Google Play). Some native apps are vendor-installed on the mobile device you purchase. One of the advantages of native apps is that they are fast in terms of performance and adjust well to their native platforms. On the other hand, they are expensive to develop, and businesses should maintain multiple versions of the app to support users across mobile devices. One way to distinguish native apps from the other types is that these apps can only be accessed through specific mobile devices. Tender (a social networking app) and Uber (a taxi-sharing app) are examples of native apps.

Web-Based Apps

Web-based apps look like natives apps, but in reality they are websites optimized for mobile access. For example, TouchStyle (a fashion design app) is a web-based app for iPad. Web-based apps are created using standard web-coding techniques (such as JavaScript or HTML5) and are accessed using Internet browsers, and are hence not available in app stores. The advantage of developing web-based apps is that they can be accessed from any mobile device and are less costly to develop and maintain. However, in terms of performance, they are not as fast and useable as the native apps. And because they are not distributed through apps stores, it is hard to monetize them.

Hybrid Apps

A hybrid app combines the functionalities of both native and web-based apps. Like native apps, they are available in app stores, and like web apps, they are developed using standard web programming languages (e.g., HTML) and then packaged up into native applications. Packaging or wrapping it into a native container makes it possible for a hybrid app to access native platform features (Korf and Oksman 2014). The Facebook app, for example, was initially a hybrid app, but later was changed to a native app. The advantage of hybrid apps is that they can be used on any mobile device, including Android, iOS, Windows Phone, and BlackBerry. This way businesses can get the advantages of native applications while keeping the cost of development lower.

From the Perspective of Objectives

Apps vary based on themes or objectives and can also be classified in terms of objectives. There are dozens of possible categories; Google Play store, for example, lists at least twenty-seven different categories of apps. Below we only discuss the most common categories.

Transaction-Oriented Apps

Transaction-oriented apps are designed to carry out virtual business transactions (such as purchasing a product or depositing money into an account) with customers. For example, eBay's app allows user to buy, sell, and manage products using their mobile devices. In a way, transaction-enabled apps provide functionality similar to an electronic commerce website's shopping cart system.

Ads-Oriented Apps

Ads-oriented apps are designed to generate revenue using advertisement banners embedded in the app. Owners provide the app for free in hopes of generating revenue by linking the user to the advertiser's website. In terms of objectives, they are similar to any other ad-based websites.

Information-Oriented Apps

These apps are designed primarily for information purposes. Companies, organizations, and sometimes ordinary people deploy these apps to help users find information about things like products, services, and facilities. These apps do not have virtual transaction abilities. Examples of information-oriented apps include toilet-finder, MyCar (for locating your car), and MapFactor (a navigation app).

Networking-Oriented Apps

Like social networking sites, networking-oriented apps are designed to facilitate social relations among people. Tender and Skout are examples of social networking apps.

Communication-Oriented Apps

These apps are used to facilities communication among users. With these apps, users can exchange text messages, pictures, and carry voice and video communication. Whatsapp, Snapchat, Viber, and Kakao Talk are examples of communication-oriented apps.

Entertainment-Oriented Apps

Entertainment-oriented apps are created for pleasure and leisure. A popular category of entertainment apps are gamming apps such as Angry Birds and Candy Crush.

Education-Oriented Apps

These apps are created for education purposes, such as learning a new skill, language, or subject. For cxample, SpeakTribe is an app for learning Spanish and Math Workout is an app for learning mathematics.

Self-Improvement Apps

Self-improvement apps are used to track or monitor oneself for a variety of purposes, including improvement of health, habits, skills, and abilities. Nike+, for example, is an app for tracking your workouts and fitness progress.

CHARACTERISTICS OF MOBILE APPS

The best way to differentiate mobile apps from desktop-based applications is through their characteristics. The following are some key characteristics that distinguish mobile apps from desktop-based applications.

ALWAYS ON

An app is always on and connected to the Internet. This makes it possible to push information and content to users as it becomes available.

MOVEABLE

Unlike the desktop applications, mobile apps goes where the user goes. Thus, it stays with the user 24/7, and users can access it anywhere and anytime.

LOCATION AWARENESS

Thanks to the GPS (global positioning system) embedded in mobile devices, apps are always aware of the user's location. The location awareness ability of apps is of great interest to social marketers, as it can be used to send target ads and promotions based on users' current location.

FOCUSED

Being focused on one theme/issue is one of the main characteristics of mobile applications that distinguish it from the desktop based applications or websites, which generally have a wider scope. There are always a narrow set of activities that an apps are designed to carry out.

PERSONALIZATION

Mobile apps can provide personalized experience based on user preferences. Users can not only control which content they prefer to see, but also how their information and data is shared, and they can store data for other purposes.

SHORT-TERM USE

Unlike desktop applications that are used for longer sessions, mobile app usage is characterized by frequent but short-term use ranging from several seconds to several minutes.

EASY TO USE

Last but not the least, mobile apps are extremely easy to use and navigate.

DEVELOPING YOUR OWN APP

Discussing app development is beyond the scope of this book. However, when it comes to having your own app, you mainly have three options.

DO-IT-YOURSELF

Get your own programmers/developers to develop one for you. Google's software development kit (SDK) for mobile analytics is a great place to start: https://developers.google.com/analytics/solutions/mobile. This way you cut some cost; however, it requires a lot of technical resources.

OUTSOURCE IT

If it is beyond your technical abilities to create an app, you may hire a company, such as BuildFire, Intellectsoft, or AppsBuilder, to do it for you. Loss of control over your app and cost of outsourcing may be an issue here.

GO OPEN SOURCE

You can also create your own business app through open-source platforms. For example, OpenMEAP™ is an open sourced mobile application platform that enables businesses with no technical skills to easily create, manage, and deploy mobile apps. Or you could deploy the PhoneGap (http://phonegap.com/) open source platform to create your own app for free.

MOBILE ANALYTICS TOOLS

Some famous mobile analytics tools are listed below.

Google Mobile Analytics: Google Mobile Analytics (http://www.google.co.kr/analytics/mobile/) is a mobile analytics tool for analyzing and tracking mobile applications data.

Countly: Countly (https://count.ly/) is a mobile application analytic tool. In this chapter, we will use the Countly analytic tool for app analysis purposes.

Mixpanel: Like Google Mobile Analytics and Countly, Mixpanel (https://mixpanel.com/) is also a mobile analytics platform.

CASE STUDY: MOBILE ANALYTICS TO OPTIMIZE PROCESS

ABOUT AIRBNB

Airbnb is a trusted community marketplace for people to list, discover, and book unique accommodations around the world—online or from a mobile phone. Whether an apartment for a night, a castle for a week, or a villa for a month, Airbnb connects people to unique travel experiences, at any price point, in more than 33,000 cities and 192 countries.

THE PROBLEM

Travelers love Airbnb, in part, due to the high number and wide variety of interesting spaces available to rent. Airbnb needed an analytics solution to help them optimize the process potential hosts go through as they list their space.

SOLUTION

Airbnb knows first-hand how difficult it is to build an analytics tool, they built their own for their website. When it came time to instrument their iPhone app, they didn't want to repeat the process, so they turned to Mixpanel (https://mixpanel.com/). Mixpanel is an advance mobile analytics tool that can provide actionable insights. Airbnb had Mixpanel up and tracking events in their iPhone app in just a couple of hours. Airbnb simply had to import the Mixpanel iPhone library into their app and add tracking calls to all of the events they wanted to analyze.

OUTCOME

Airbnb didn't just optimize their first time listing and booking flows, they also used Mixpanel to measure where their customers spent the most time within the app, their most frequent actions, and the percentage of people who passively browsed vs. actively managed a booking.

Airbnb used Mixpanel's event tracking and funnel analysis to keep tabs on everything they wanted to measure. Particularly important was funnel analysis, which they used extensively to optimize the listing process for first time hosts. Based on the drop-offs they found in Mixpanel, Airbnb revamped host listing process on their app, resulting in a 400% increase in conversion rate.

Source: Mixpanel, *https://mixpanel.com/*

TUTORIAL: APPS ANALYTICS WITH COUNTLY

Countly is innovative, real-time mobile analytics software, focusing on ease of use, extensibility, and feature richness. Countly includes a server and a mobile component, both of which you can freely use in your own company for your applications under license terms.

The server part of Countly consists of a service that runs on port 80, allowing the system administrator to connect to the user interface and get insights about applications tracked. The mobile part consists of SDKs for different smartphones and tablets (e.g., Android and iOS). In order to start tracking your application, you need to do the following:

1. Choose a compliant server operating system (e.g., Ubuntu 10.04 or later).
2. Install the server application so it's ready to collect data.
3. Put the SDK in your application.
4. Put the application on your mobile phone and test.
5. If the tests are successful, send the application to the Apple Store/Google Play.

Installation of the server application and using SDK is explained in documents you can find on the navigation bar on the left, and is beyond the scope of this guide. Detailed installation instructions can also be found on Countly's resources page: http://resources.count.ly/. You can also download an up-to-date Countlly tutorial with several screenshots from the book companion site: http://7layersanalytics.com/.

After all steps are completed, you are ready to get insights from your Countly dashboard. You can also get familiar with the tool by accessing its online demo available here: http://sentio.count.ly/dashboard#/

DASHBOARD OVERVIEW

Countly provides a dashboard for a quick glimpse of the latest status of application usage. In the dashboard you will notice the following (Screenshot 14):

1. Navigation bar
2. Real-time panel
3. Quick date selector
4. Engagement
5. Analytics panel
6. Events
7. Drills
8. Funnels
9. Revenue analytics panel

The options you see may vary based on the version you are subscribed to. Currently, Countly is available in three levels: 1) professional, 2) business, and 3) enterprise. Below we explain common options available on the dashboard.

Navigation Bar

At the top of the navigation bar, you'll see a list of applications. Each can be selected at once, and the dashboard will adapt itself showing numbers for the selected application. "Dashboard" is the initial view, and the Analytics menu includes several other views that can be of interest, including detailed carrier, country, user-retention, and session frequency metrics. User and application management are also carried out using links here. At the bottom of this part, you can see the current user, together with a link to log out and a password change option.

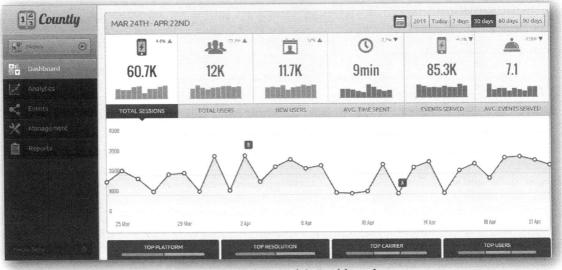

Screenshot 14 Countly's Dashboard

Real-Time Panel

Have you ever wondered how many users are currently using your application at that moment? This tiny but powerful widget shows you exactly that: online users and incoming online users. There's also a live flowchart on the right-hand side that shows the status of your users—you can easily get insight into whether the numbers of online and new users are increasing and decreasing. The real-time panel is only available for business and enterprise edition users.

Quick Date Selector

On the top right of the screen you'll see a list of dates. Here, you can either use a defined time frame or select a date from the time selector. Note that if you select a time here, it'll be automatically selected as you click on other navigation links (e.g., "Users," "Carriers," etc.). In order to select a date, click on the selector, choose start and finish dates, and click on "Apply." Graphs and corresponding boxed widgets will automatically be updated.

Analytics Panel

This panel gives a brief overview of what's happening on the dashboard. On the top, there are six widgets. When clicked, the charts under these widgets are automatically refreshed to show relevant data groups.

Each widget shows the following:

1. **Total sessions:** Number of times your application is opened. Click this item to see a time series representation of total sessions.
2. **Total users:** Number of unique devices your application is used from. Click this item to see a time series representation of total users.
3. **New users:** Number of first-time users. Click this item to see a time series representation of new users.
4. **Time spent:** Total time spent on your application. Click this item to see a time series representation of total time spent per user.
5. **Average time spent:** Total time spent using your application divided by total user count. Click this item to see a time series representation of average time spent per user.
6. **Average requests received:** Number of written API requests the Countly server received for this application divided by total user count. Click this item to see a time series representation of average events per user.

For each time series chart, there is a light gray and dark gray line. The light gray line shows the previous time frame for comparison purposes.

GETTING IN-DEPTH ANALYTICS

Countly's dashboard provides a quick analysis and gives a glimpse of how your application is performing. It's mostly useful for marketing people who want to understand what's going on immediately.

The navigation pane on the left gives more detailed information about users, sessions, countries, carriers, and more. Below we'll have a look at each menu item.

Users—The "Users" tab is one of the most important part of the analytics. Here you'll see an overview of total, new, and returning users based on day. This is the menu you'll need to keep track of most. This tab will give you the answer to the question, "How many users do I have?"

Sessions—If the user opens an application, it counts as a session until he closes it. This menu shows an overview of sessions, together with total sessions, unique sessions, and new sessions, broken down by time. This menu will give you the answer to the question, "How many times has your application been opened?"

Countries—This menu gives an overview of which countries your applications are used in most. It will show the world map, total users, total sessions, and new users. This menu will give you the answer to the question, "Where do my users connect from?"

Devices—In this menu, you'll see three main blocks of device information. On the top, there's a list of devices, and at the bottom, these devices are shown in a table. In the middle, there are three blocks of information, showing the top platform, top operating system version, and top resolution, respectively. Try hovering on each color line and you'll see other top information. This menu will give you the answer to the question, "Which smartphone types do my users have?"

Resolutions—This menu shows two pie charts illustrating total users and new users in terms of device resolution (width x height). This is important as it gives insights about which resolutions are used most so you can focus on these screen types.

Density—Android devices have screen densities, and this menu shows densities reported by device. This menu is only for Android applications.

Application versions—This page shows different versions of applications, in case they are defined. A stacked chart shows total sessions and new users. The table under the chart shows total sessions, total users, and new users, respectively for each application version. This menu will give you the answer to the question, "How do my application versions compare?"

Carriers—The "Carriers" page shows a table of all carriers, together with total sessions, total users, and new users for a given period. On the top of the page, there are two pie charts showing total users and new users of top carriers. There are only three carriers shown in this chart for compatibility, so refer to the table for a detailed carrier breakdown. This menu will give you the answer to the question, "Which operator do they use?"

Platforms—Countly provides an intuitive interface to show how different platforms (operating systems) perform. If you use the same app key ("Management→Applications"), it's possible to aggregate this information and see it under this menu. This menu will give you the answer to the question, "Which operating systems do my users have?"

Engagement View

This menu includes submenu items related to user engagement, such as retention, loyalty, session frequency, and session duration.

User retention—Retention is the condition of keeping your customers. This page shows you active days (e.g., days your customers used your application) after the first session. In the top right corner, you can get a breakdown of daily, weekly, and monthly retention. This is one of the most important metrics for app analytics.

User loyalty—User loyalty shows how many users started a specific number of sessions. The table shows the number and percentage of each loyalty group compared with number of sessions (e.g., one session, two sessions, and so forth). This menu will give you the answer to the question, "How many users started a specific number of sessions?"

Session frequency—Session frequency shows how often you see your mobile users open your application. It can be used to calculate the trends, or how often your application is used during a given period of time. The session frequency graph is very straightforward: you'll see a breakdown of number of sessions and corresponding number and percentage of users for each group. Most of the time, you will see that many users will be accumulated in the "first session" and "second session" row. This menu will give you the answer to the question, "How often do you see your users open your app?"

Session durations—The "Session Durations" view shows users categorized into predefined session duration buckets. In this view, your users are categorized into one of 0–0 seconds, 11–30 seconds, 31–60 seconds, 1–3 minutes, 3–10 minutes, 10–30 minutes, 30–60 minutes or >1 hour, according to this session duration. This screen will give you the answer to the question, "How long do my users stay inside my application?"

Events

Countly provides a way to create custom events based on user needs. An event can be anything that managers want to measure and track, such as tracking user navigation patterns and purchase behavior). With custom events, you may be able to answer business intelligence questions such as:

- What item is purchased most?
- Which countries were top performers in terms of in-app purchases?
- Which application version leads to more sales?

It helps business managers to get an understanding how their application performs by sending data from inside the application and analyzing this information. Just like other information retrieved, custom events are true real-time.

More information on how to create custom events is available on the Countly's resources page: http://resources.count.ly/

Funnels

Funnels are used to track the goal completion rates of a step-by-step path inside your application. Funnels can, for example, be used for:

- Ranking in-app purchase conversions, understanding the paths that lead to IAPs, and optimizing them
- Understanding which level or part of your application users tend to leave
- Performing A/B test analysis to see which versions perform better.

These goals (steps) are defined as custom events in Countly, and you don't need any extra/new API calls if you have already been using custom events.

Step 1: Click on the funnels available at left bottom section. The first time you open the funnels view, you will be greeted by a funnel creation form. Here you can define the steps of your funnel by either inputting the custom event key you plan to send in the future or selecting one from your existing events. A funnel needs to have at least two steps.

Step 2: After saving your funnel, you will immediately be taken to your reporting view. At the top you can see how many users of your application entered this funnel by performing the first step event. Right next to it there is the success rate and number of users who have completed this funnel by performing every single event.

Step 3: You can filter the first step event by your event's segmentation properties as well as user properties (metrics) like platform, device, country, etc.

Applications and Users

Countly provides a user interface to manage applications and system users.

Managing applications—Applications can be managed by global users (more information on users is provided later). To add an application, follow the steps below:

1. Go to "Management→ Applications."
2. Click on the "Add" option.
3. Enter your application name, category, the time zone you are in, and upload your application icon.
4. Click "Add Application."

You'll be given an app key that is unique to that application. This key should be written in the SDK code snippet, which in turn will be embedded in your application. For more details, refer to the County's resources website: http://resources.count.ly/.

Alternatively, you can enter your IAP Event Key in order to collect IAP revenues and see it immediately in your dashboard.

If you want to delete an application, simply click on "Delete." There may be some cases where you want to delete all data associated with an application, but keep the application keys and other information. In this case, use "Clear data" to remove all incoming data from this application and start fresh.

Managing users—Countly provides a way to manage different types of users (e.g., global admin, admin, or user). Each user will be able to see the privileges assigned to them. For example, you may want your marketing team to be able to see the whole dashboard, whereas the website manager, as the global admin, can easily add/remove applications, define other users, and manage whole interfaces. Different types of users have different authorization levels:

1. **Global admins** can add/remove/edit users, add/remove/edit applications and typically can do whatever is assigned them on the user interface. This is the most powerful user.
2. **Admins** can manage applications, for example, add, edit, or remove an application completely from the management dashboard. If you are the global admin and your organization controls other sub-organizations or companies, then you'll probably want to add different admins to manage different applications.
3. **Users** are basically at the bottom of the hierarchy, and can only see the dashboard, without having the ability to manage other applications and users.

In order to add a user, you must be a global admin. Click "Create a new user" to get a dropdown menu where you can enter user information and credentials. Fill in the details here and click "Create user." Editing a user is straightforward: Go to the user row and click. You'll be presented with an editable form.

Revenue Analytics Panel

Countly offers revenue analytics to Countly Cloud and Enterprise users for tracking in-app–purchase (IAP) data in real time. Revenue analytics provide the following information:

- Total revenue
- Average revenue per user
- Average revenue per paying user
- Paying user count
- Paying/total users

In order to make revenue analytics, you need to define an in-app—purchase event. Define an event as follows.

1. Go to "Management→ Applications."
2. Click "Edit."
3. Select an AIP event key by typing the event name.
4. Click "Save Changes."

Changing Interface Language

Countly is available in several languages, including German, Spanish, Turkish, Italian, Dutch, Russian, Chinese, and more. You can easily switch languages from the menu on left-hand side. Click on your name and then the language button, where you'll see available languages.

Source: Countly, *https://count.ly/*

Review Questions

1. Briefly explain the two main categories of mobile analytics.
2. What is the purpose of apps analytics?
3. Briefly explain the different classes of mobile apps.
4. What are some main characteristics of mobile apps?
5. Briefly explain the different app development options.

CHAPTER 7

SOCIAL MEDIA HYPERLINK ANALYTICS

HYPERLINKS ARE the pathways of social media traffic. Hyperlinks are references to web resources (such as a website, document, and files) that users can access by clicking on it. Hyperlinks can link resources within a document (inter-linking) and among documents (intralinking). For example, clicking on a hyperlink in a tweet can link you to other resources (e.g., websites) available over the Internet.

Hyperlinks are not merely technical links between two websites, but serve a more symbolic means (Park 2003; Kim and Nam 2012). As a website is an official and unique entity representing an organization itself (Garrido 2003); therefore, embedding hyperlinks in an organization's website can be considered an official act of communication between two organizations. Hyperlinks among websites represent not only a reasonable approximation of a social relationship (Jackson 1997), but also serve as a symbolic meaning of validating or endorsing the linked organization (Vreelnad 2000). In conjunction with this, these hyperlinks that exist between two organizational websites reflect a sense a sense of validation, trust, bonding, authority, and legitimacy (Vreelnad 2000; Park 2003; Nam, Barnett et al. 2014). Websites mostly connect or link to other websites of similar nature, so hyperlinks can also serves as indicators of content similarity (Chakrabarti, Joshi et al. 2002).

TYPES OF HYPERLINKS

From hyperlink analytics point of view, mainly there are three types of hyperlinks, 1) in-links, 2) out-links, and 3) co-links.

IN-LINKS

In-links are the incoming hyperlinks or links directed toward a website or originated in other websites (Björneborn and Ingwersen 2004). For example, consider the top left image in the Figure 9, page A is receiving two in-links coming from pages B and C.

In-links are of great interest to social markers, because they bring traffic to a particular website. Thus, harvesting them can help us understand where the traffic to a corporate website is coming from. In-links also play an important role in website analytics, as both the quality and number of in-links can impact the search engine ranking of the website (more details on this are provided in the search analytics chapter). (Thelwall 2001) In-links can also impact the popularity of social media contents. A study on YouTube viral videos, for instance, found that among other things, in-links play crucial roles in the viral phenomenon, particularly in increasing views of videos posted on YouTube (Khan and Vong 2014). Studies have also shown that in-link counts strongly correlate with measures describing business performance (Vaughan 2004).

Out-Links

Out-links are hyperlinks generated out of a website (Bjorneborn 2001). As shown in the top-right image in the Figure 9, page A is sending two out-links: one to page B and one to page C.

Co-Links

Co-links have two dimensions. First, if two websites receive a link from a third website, they are considered to be connected indirectly. For example, page A links to both pages B and C, therefore B and C are considered to be co-linking, or connected indirectly (bottom-left image in the Figure 9).

Second, if two pages link to a third page, they are also considered to be co-linking. As shown in the bottom-right corner of the Figure 9, Pages B and C are linking to page A; therefore, B and C are connected indirectly. Co-links have been used to compare and map competitive similarity among companies (Vaughan and You 2006).

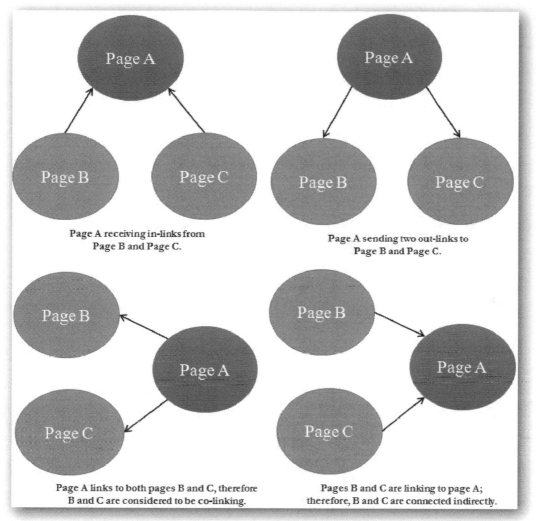

Figure 9. Different types of hyperlinks

HYPERLINK ANALYTICS

Hyperlink analytics deals with extracting, analyzing, and interpreting hyperlinks (e.g., in-links, out-links, and co-links). The basic assumption pertaining to hyperlink analytics is that the number and quality of hyperlinks to a website equates to its importance or value (Thelwall 2014). Hyperlink analytics can also reveal, for example, Internet traffic patterns and sources of the incoming or outgoing traffic to and from a website. Hyperlink analysis has been used to study a variety of topics including ranking of universities, understanding the blogosphere, scholarly websites (Vaughan and Thelwall 2003), and political networks (Park and Thelwall 2008), and to measure business competitiveness (Vaughan and You

2006). The case study included in this chapter demonstrates the importance of hyperlinks in viral phenomena and shows the valuable insights they carry for viral marketers in formulating viral marketing strategies. We must admit that, regardless of its importance, hyperlink analysis also has some limitations. Hyperlink networks, for example, does not provide any insight into the type or amount of traffic flowing among websites(Ackland 2010).

When we talk about hyperlinks analytics, it mostly implies in-links, out-links, and co-links analysis and does not include hyperlinks within a website between pages. Hyperlinks between pages within a website are created mostly for navigational purposes. Also, search engine ranking algorithms either ignore or give low importance to hyperlinks within a website (Thelwall 2014).

TYPES OF HYPERLINK ANALYTICS

Hyperlink analytics can take several forms, including: 1) hyperlink environment analysis, 2) link impact analysis, and 3) social media hyperlink analysis.

Hyperlink Environment Analysis

Hyperlink environment analyses deal with a particular website or set of websites. Hyperlinks (i.e., out-links, in-links, and co-links) of a website are extracted and analyzed to identify the sources of Internet traffic. Hyperlinks environment networks can take two forms: 1) co-links networks or 2) in-links and out-links networks.

Co-Link Networks

In co-links environment networks, nodes are websites and links that represent similarity between websites, as measured by co-link counts. With the Webometric Analyst tool, one can construct a co-link network diagram among a set of websites (Thelwall 2005; Thelwall 2014).

In-Links and Out-Links Networks

In-links and out-links hyperlink environment networks are constructed based on in-links and out-links from a website or set of websites. In such a network, nodes will be websites and links will present in-links and out-links. The tutorial provided in this chapter demonstrates constructs such as network using the VOSON hyperlink analysis tool.

Link Impact Analysis

Link impact analysis investigates the web impact of a website address (or URL) in terms of citations or mentions it receives over the web. In a link impact analysis, statistics about web pages that mention the URL of a given website are collected and analyzed (Thelwall 2005; Thelwall 2014). The assumption is that a URL (or website address) cited frequently over the web is more important. Thus, measuring the web impact of URLs may provide an idea about the importance of a website.

Social Media Hyperlink Analysis

Social media hyperlink analysis deals with extraction and analysis of hyperlinks embedded within social media texts (.e.g., tweets and comments). These hyperlinks can be extracted and studied to identify the sources and destination of social media traffic. A good example of the usefulness of the hyperlink embedded in the social media text is the study by Khan et al. (2014), in which they extracted out-links from Korean and US government agencies' tweets. By extracting out-links and tracing them back to their sender, the authors were able to constructed a map of the out-link structure (Figure 10). According to a comparison of out-links between tweets of the Korean and US governments, there were some differences in citation (i.e., out-link) patterns. The Korean government tended to cite domestic portals' news services and their own blogs (i.e., self-citation). Although there were SNSs and newspaper sites, most of the related out-links were for portals. On the other hand, the US government showed a more diverse pattern in terms of out-link destinations. US out-links were not concentrated in specific sites and tended to go directly to news agencies, not to secondary sources such as portals. These comparisons between the US and Korean governments suggest that social media out-links can carry valuable information and can help explain real-world phenomena and shed light on the disparities in social media use among different cultures (Khan, Yoon et al. 2014).

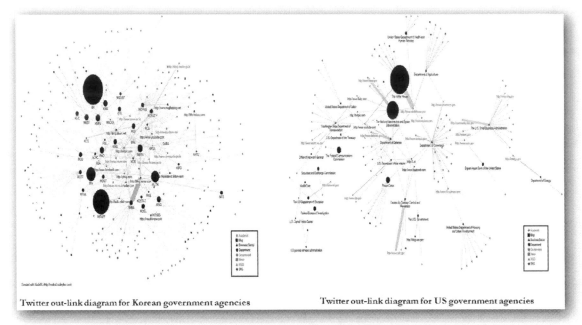

Figure 10. Twitter networks for Korea (left) and the US Governments (right)

HYPERLINK ANALYTICS TOOLS

The following are some popular hyperlink analytics tools.

Webometric Analyst: Webometric Analyst is a web impact analysis tool and can conduct variety of analysis on social media platforms including hyperlink network analysis and web mentions: http://lexiurl.wlv.ac.uk/

VOSON: VOSON (http://www.uberlink.com/) is a hyperlink analytics tools for constructing and analyzing hyperlink networks. More details on VOSON are provided in the hyperlink analytics chapter. This chapter includes a detailed tutorial on using VOSON for hyperlink analysis.

Open Site Explorer: Open Site Explorer is a link analysis tool to research and compare competitor backlinks, identify top pages, view social activity data, and analyze anchor text: https://moz.com/researchtools/ose/

Link Diagnosis: Link Diagnosis (http://www.linkdiagnosis.com/) is a free online tool for analyzing and diagnosing links.

Advanced Link Manager: Advanced Link Manager provides a variety of link analysis capabilities, including the ability to track link-building progress over time, domain quality analysis, backlinks evolution, and website-crawling abilities: http://www.advancedlinkmanager.com/

Majestic: Majestic (https://majestic.com) provides a variety of link analysis tools, including link explorer, backlinks history, and link mapping tools.

Backlink Watch: Backlink Watch (http://backlinkwatch.com/) is a free tool for checking the quality and quantity of in-links pointing to a website.

CASE STUDY: HYPERLINKS AND VIRAL YOUTUBE VIDEOS

BACKGROUND

Do hyperlinks play a role in the popularity of a video posted over YouTube? This was the questions that a research team at *Centre for Social Technologies* (a research center dedicated to understanding social technologies: http://centreforsocialtech.com/) set out to explore. The research team knew that the answer lies in extracting and visualizing hyperlinks (particularly in-links pointing to a video) network and was looking for ways to get hands on YouTube videos data.

WHAT THEY DID

At the first stage of the quest the research team identified 100 most viewed YouTube videos. Every video posted on YouTube is automatically assigned a unique ID embedded within the URL of the video. For example, this www.youtube.com/watch?v=kffacxfA7G4 is the URL of a video posted by the user "Justin Bieber" having an ID "kffacxfA7G4." The data were collected for all the 100 video and saved it in a text file one ID per line. At the second stage, in order to explore the effects of hyperlinks on the viral phenomenon, the team turned to Webometrics Analyst (http://lexiurl.wlv.ac.uk/)—a well-established tool for measuring different aspects of the web, such as, web impact analysis, hyperlinks analysis, and web search engine results (Thelwall 2005). Using the IDs text file as an input, through Webometrics Analyst, the search team harvested the number of external links and Internet domains pointing to a video. This data was used to construct a two-mode network diagrams (Figure 11) for better understanding using UCINET social networking tool. Figure 11 shows the network of YouTube videos and the domain names pointing to YouTube videos.

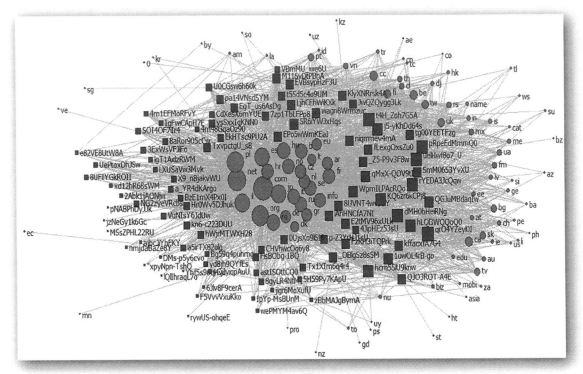

Figure 11. Viral Videos hyperlink network

In the Figure 11, the squares indicate unique videos IDs and circle nodes indicate the domain names. The links among nodes are URLs (in-link) received by the videos and users from a specific domain (arrow heads pointing from a domain toward a video or user are removed for the sake of clarity). In the case of the videos IDs, the size of a node indicates the number of URLs (in-links) received by the videos (the size of a node is bigger when it received more URLs) and in case of the domain names it means the number of out-link the domains are sending to the videos (the size is bigger when a domain sent more URLs). Width of the links among the nodes indicates the number of URLs sent a by a domain to a video: width is bigger when more URLs are sent by a domain.

RESULTS

It is clear from the Figure 11 that most of the videos received URLs from a common set of domains (as shown by the circle nodes in the middle of the figure); however, the number of URLs received are different that is, some videos received more URLs than others and some domains (e.g., com, net, and org) sent more links compared to others. The important point to note is the diversity domains received by some videos (as shown on the right side of the Figure 11). For example, the videos on the right side of the Figure 11 have not only attracted URLs from the common set of domains (e.g., com, net, and org), but also from several other diverse domains (e.g., tv, ca, sk, uk, be, tw, fi, cc). The difference among the videos receiving several diverse domain and links (as indicated by the size of the nodes on the right side of the Figure 11) vs., the videos receiving limited number of links (shown on the left side of the Figure 11) is quite visible.

CONCLUSION

This analysis shows that apart from the popularity inside YouTube system the most popular videos had a strong in-links network (links received by videos and users) originating from diverse domains over the Internet. In other words, the most popular videos on YouTube are quite visible over the Internet and these network dynamics or Internet structural capital might be one of the reasons that the videos posted by certain users go viral. This case study demonstrated the importance of hyperlinks and the valuable insights it carry it. The important implication for viral marketers here is that in-links should be taken into account while formulating virality strategies. For example, linking the videos/contents posted over the YouTube in several external platforms (e.g., blogs, social network sites, and online discussion communities) may increase its chances of getting viral and getting viral faster.

Source: compiled from Khan, G. F., Sokha, V., (2014), Virality over YouTube: an Empirical Analysis, Internet Research, Vol. 24, Issue 5.

TUTORIAL: HYPERLINKS ANALYTICS WITH VOSON

Before you continue, we suggest you review the basic social network concepts discussed in the network analytics chapter.

VOSON is a web-based tool for hyperlink network analysis. To construct and analyze hyperlink networks, VOSON relies on web mining, data visualization, and traditional social science techniques, such as social network analysis (Ackland 2010). VOSON is freely available to academics, researchers, consultants, government entities, and others outside of academia. This tutorial is based on the free version. You can also download an up-to-date VOSON tutorial with several screenshots from the book companion site: http://7layersanalytics.com/.

CREATE AN ACCOUNT

Step 1: To access the VOSON, you must first create an account by visiting this link: http://www.uberlink.com and click on the "create a new account" option available at the top of the page.

Step 2: Once you have created a username and password by filling in the appropriate form, log in to the system. After your account is approved, you will be able to start using the tool.

LOGGING IN TO VOSON

Note that currently there are two identical versions of the VOSON System. One is called VOSON@ANU and other is called VOSON@Uberlink. Each version is accessed from slightly different locations. So, first you need to find out the version you're subscribed to.

To find out which version of VOSON you have been granted access to, use the following steps.

- ✓ Go to http://www.uberlink.com and login with your username and password.
- ✓ Click on the *My Account* option available at the top of the website.
- ✓ Scroll down to the bottom of your profile, where you should see the version you are subscribed to.
- ✓ If you have access to VOSON@ANU, log in to the VOSON System at: http://voson.anu.edu.au/voson-system.
- ✓ If you have access to VOSON@Uberlink, log in to the VOSON System at: https://voson.uberlink.com.au.

VOSON MENUS

After logging into VOSON for the first time, you are presented with the following active menu items (there are many other menus that are not active and only become active when they are needed) (Screenshot 15). Details on the description of all menus can be found in the VOSON documentation available here: http://www.uberlink.com/software#voson-system.

Screenshot 15. VOSON's user interface

Info

User—This gives information on your access privileges and the projects that you belong to (and therefore what data are available to you).

Data

DataBrowser—This allows you to see the data, where each row is a web page.

    Save database—Use this to save copies of the database.

    Add seed sites—Use this to add more seed sites to the database (seed sites are used to create hyperlink networks).

    Download—Use this to access the data for viewing in other software; for example, Excel.

    Show databases—This lists all the databases that you have access to. Initially, there are only two databases available to you: testdb and testdbAN. You can use these databases to get familiar with the tool.

    Furthermore, in the VOSON System there are mainly two databases types: 1) VOSON databases and 2) VOSON-analysis databases. VOSON databases are the "parent" from which VOSON-analysis databases are created. VOSON databases contain the raw network data; whereas, VOSON-analysis databases are used to conduct network analysis such as crosstabs and network visualization.

Create

VOSON database—this menu is used to create a VOSON database.

    VOSON analysis database—this menu is used to create a VOSON analysis database.

Help

This provides two submenus for accessing documentation and information about the software.

CREATING A HYPERLINK NETWORK

Now let's shift our focus to creating a hyperlink network.

Step 1: After login, the first thing you need to do is to create a database. To create a database, click on the "Data" tab, click "Create" and then click on "VOSON database." (Screenshot 16).

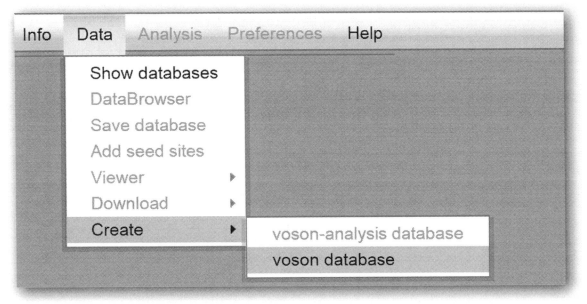

Screenshot 16. VOSON Data tab

Step 2: Provide the requested information (e.g., database name and description). Leave the other options on their default setting. The default options will perform the following tasks:

- The crawler will look for inbound links.
  - o   For each seed, the crawler stops when it discovers one thousand in-links.
  - o   The crawler will not look for inbound links to each internal page.
- The crawler will look for outbound links.
  - o   For each seed, the crawler will stop when it discover one thousand out-links.

- It will crawl twenty-five pages without finding a new outbound link (the maximum number of unproductive pages).
- It will crawl only fifty pages (the depth of crawl in pages).
- It will crawled two levels (the depth of crawl in levels).
- The text content will not be parsed.

Step 3: The database is now created.

Step 4: Now you will notice that other submenus within the "Data" menu have become active. To create a network, click on the "Data" menu, click on "Create," and then on "VOSON analysis database."

Step 5: Provide a name for database. Select "Hyperlinks" in the "Link type" and "pagegroup" in the "Node Type" dropdown boxes. Click "Create database." This database will be used to construct our hyperlink network.

Step 6: Now is time to add seed sites that will be used to create the hyperlink network. For this tutorial, we used http://www.uberlink.com/ as the seed site, but you can use the website address of your company. You can add several seed sites, but the total number of seed sites you can add depends on your subscription plan. To add the site, first click on your newly created database to activate it. Then click on "Data," then on "Add Seed Sites."

A new window will be opened. Type the URL of your company's website in the box provided. Leave other options on their default settings and click on the "Add" button next to the comment box (which you can use to add comments, if you have any).

Now check the "ready to crawl" box. A popup window will alert you about the status of credit and number of credits needed to perform the crawl. Click "OK" to start the process.

Note that the sites will not be crawled immediately; you will receive an e-mail when the crawling has finished.

Step 7: After you have received the e-mail from VOSON informing you that the data set is ready, click on "Data>Show databases." Now your database has been populated with data (e.g., thirty-one rows).

Step 8: To check the network properties of your hyperlink network, first click on the database (VOSON-analysis type) to make it active. Then, click on the "Analysis" tab and then click on "SNA."

Step 9: A new window will open summarizing in detail the properties of the network, including the following (most of these concepts were discussed in the network analytics chapter).

Size—the total of number of websites (or nodes) in the network.

Number of edges—the total number of hyperlinks (in-links and out-links) among the websites.

Components—the isolated sub-networks that connect within, but are disconnected between networks (Hanneman and Riddle 2005).

Density—the *density* of a network deals with a number of links in a network.

Number of isolates—the number of nodes that have no connections to other nodes.

Inclusiveness—the proportion of the nodes in the network that are connected.

Step 10: To visualize the hyperlink network, click on the "Analysis" tab, and then "Maps," and then select one of the three available options: "Minimum spanning tree," "Complete network," or "Hierarchy" (depending on the version of VOSON you're using, you may see more options). These are in fact network visualization algorithms, and each one will visualize the network differently. We selected the "Complete Network," which show all links and nodes simultaneously.

Step 11: The hyperlink network will appear in a separate window (Screenshot 17). You can easily notice the out-links and in-links by looking at the arrowheads. If the arrowhead points to the seed site, it is an in-link, and if it points away, it is an out-link from the seed site to another website. The countries where the hyperlinks are coming from are shown on the right hand side. You can redraw the network based on several parameters shown in the upper part of the window. For example, we configured the node size based on the in-degree (i.e., the number of incoming hyperlinks). The node size will be bigger if a website has more in-links. Clicking on a specific node will display more details about the node.

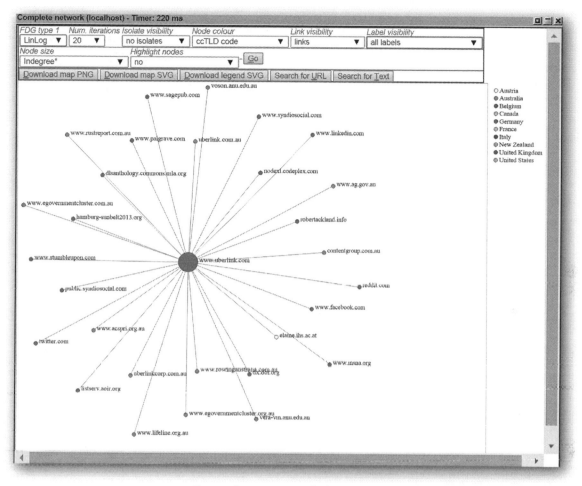

Screenshot 17. Hyperlink network

Step 12: To save the network diagram, click on "download map PNG" and save it on your computer.

Step 13: You can also export the network data to be used with other network analysis software (e.g., Pajek and GrapML). To do so, click on "Data," then "Download" and then select the format you want to download the data in.

Review Questions

1. What are hyperlinks, and why they are important?
2. Briefly discuss in-links, out-links, and co-links.
3. What is hyperlink analytics and its underlying assumptions?
4. What is hyperlink environment analysis?
5. What is link impact analysis?
6. What is social media hyperlink analysis?

CHAPTER 8

LOCATION ANALYTICS

LOCATION ANALYTICS, also known as spatial analysis or geo-analytics is concerned with mapping, visualizing, and mining the location of people, data, and other resources. All sectors, including business, government, nonprofit, and academia, can benefit from location analytics. The case study "Owl Bus" included in this chapter demonstrates how location analytics and social media helped Seoul Metropolitan Government in expanding their bus routes and selecting the "Owl Bus" brand name. Thanks to the GPS (global positioning systems) embedded in mobile devices, providing location-based services, products, and information is becoming a reality. In a recent study, scientists used six million geo-located Twitter messages to observe the "heartbeat" of New York City (França, Sayama et al. 2015). Using the dataset, the scientist were able to study and map the waking, sleeping, commuting, work, and leisure dynamics of the people living in the city during the weekday and weekends. Such geo-analytics can be instrumental in better understanding our cities and human behaviors in space and time.

Sources of Location Data
Location information can come from a variety of sources, including the following.

Postal Address
Most business analytics applications rely on address information of their customers, including city names, locality names, and postal or zip codes.

Latitude and Longitude
In geography, latitude (shown as a horizontal line on a globe) and longitude (shown as a vertical line on a globe) are used to find exact location on Earth.

GPS-BASED

GPS is a satellite-based navigation system that can be used find exact location people and resources. Mobile analytics mostly rely on GPS-based location data. GPS-based location analytics can provide us the most accurate location for social media users.

IP-BASED

Public IP (Internet protocol) can be used to determine the location of Internet users. A public IP address is an exclusive numerical address (like a home address) assigned to a device connected to the Internet. Different regions in the world are assigned a specific block of public IP addresses; hence, it can be used to mine approximate geo-location of Internet users.

CATEGORIES OF LOCATION ANALYTICS

Based on its scope, location analytics can be broadly classified into two categories: 1) business data-driven location analytics, 2) social media data-driven location analytics.

BUSINESS DATA-DRIVEN LOCATION ANALYTICS

Business data-driven location analytics deals with mapping, visualizing, and mining location data to reveal patterns, trends, and relationships hidden in tabular business data. Capitalizing on the data stored in a business database, location analytics, for example, can map and capture vast among of geo-specific data to provide information, products, and services based on where customers are. Using the location of customers, for instance, it is possible to recommend the nearest convenience store, coffee shop, taxi, or even probable social relations. Or it can be used for any other business decision, such as, what is the best potential new site for a business warehouse?

Applications of Business Data-Driven Location Analytics

Business data-driven location analytics has several applications, including the following.

Powerful Intelligence

Simple maps have been widely used, but they are limited in providing insightful details. Using sophisticated mapping techniques, such as clustering, heat mapping, data aggregation (e.g., aggregating data to regions), and color-coded mapping, can generate powerful business intelligence (Hecht 2013).

Geo-Enrichment

Simple data maps can be enriched with customer data, including demographic, consumer spending, lifestyle, and locations (Hecht 2013). For example, where do my loyal customers spend most of their time?

Collaboration and Sharing

Maps are easy to understand and are good communication and collaboration tools. Location analytics can map business data for collaboration across organization. It can also be used for information sharing purposes with customers. At end of this chapter, a step-by-step tutorial is provided to map sample tabular business data using Google Fusion Tables. With Google Fusion Tables, you can map data and display and share the results as maps, tables, and charts.

SOCIAL MEDIA DATA-DRIVEN LOCATION ANALYTICS

Social media data-driven analytics relies on social media location data to mine and map location of social media users, content, and data. Social media location information comes mainly from GPS and IP.

Uses of Social Media-Based Location Analytics

Social media location–based services are becoming a day-to-day reality. Organizations use location-based services for a variety of purposes, including the following.

Recommendation Purposes

Organizations can harvest location data to recommend products, services, and social events to potential customers in real time as they approach certain localities. For example, Tender recommends potential social relationships based on the location of users.

Customer Segmentation

Social media location data can be used to segment customers based on their geographic location. Tweepsmap (https://tweepsmap.com/), for example, can be used to geo-locate your Twitter followers by country, state, or city.

Advertisement

Location-based advertisement allows targeted marketing and promotion campaign mostly delivered through mobile devices to reach specific target audiences.

Information Request

Based on their current location, customers can request a product, service, or resource (e.g., the nearest coffee shop, restaurant, or parking lot).

Alerts

Location data can be used to send and receive alerts and notifications, such as sales and promotion alerts traffic congestion alerts, speed limit warnings, and storm warnings.

Search and Rescue

Location data is vital in search and rescue operations. For example, Agos a geo-tagging and reporting platform that enables communities deal with climate change adaptation and disaster risk reduction.

Navigation

Mobile- and GPS-based navigation services and apps assist us in finding addresses. BE-ON-ROAD, for instance, is a free offline turn-by-turn GPS navigation app for Android devices.

LOCATION ANALYTICS AND PRIVACY CONCERNS

While location-based services bring ease, convenience, and safety to customers and value to business, they also raise serious privacy issues related to collection, retention, use, and disclosure of location information (Minch 2004). Tracking, mining, and storing location information can endanger some fundamental human rights, such as freedom of movement and freedom from being observed. Minch (2004) raised several issues arising from location-based services, including the following.

- Should users of location-enabled devices be informed when location tracking is in use?
- Should users of location-enabled devices be permitted to control the storage of location information?
- Should location information as stored be personally identifiable, or should the user have the option to preserve degrees of anonymity?
- What legal protection should a person's historical location information have against unreasonable search and seizure?
- To what extent should users of location-based services be allowed to choose their own level of identifiability/anonymity?
- What level of disclosure control should be dictated by government regulation? By the affected individual customers, users, etc.? By other parties?
- What governmental legislation and regulation is appropriate to assure citizens' rights of privacy in an era of location-aware mobile devices?

LOCATION ANALYTICS TOOLS

Google Fusion Tables: Google Fusion Tables is a web service to geo-tag, store, share, query, and visualize tabular business data overlaid on Google Maps. This chapter provides a detailed tutorial on Google Fusion Tables.

Agos: Agos is a geo-tagging and reporting platform that helps communities deal with climate change adaptation and disaster risk reduction: http://agos.rappler.com/#

Tweepsmap: Tweepsmap (https://tweepsmap.com/) maps your Twitter followers by country, state, or city.

Trendsmap: Trendsmap (http://trendsmap.com/) is real-time tool that maps the latest trends from Twitter, anywhere in the world.

Followerwonk: This tool helps you perform basic Twitter analytics, such as, who are your followers? Where are they located? When do they tweet? The tool can be accessed via http://followerwonk.com/

Esri: Esri's GIS (geographic information systems) is software to map, visualize, question, analyze, and interpret data to understand relationships, patterns, and trends (http://www.esri.com/).

Case Study: the "Owl Bus"

Background

The Seoul Night Bus, also known as the "Owl Bus," is the brand name of the Seoul (South Korea) city's intracity buses that run nine routes exclusively from midnight to 5:00 a.m. Like an owl, animated in the dark with its yellow-glowing eyes, the "Owl Bus" was born to make Seoul's public transportation service ceaseless, carrying the city's late night commuters. As the service is the first of its kind in Korea, policymakers struggled to shape action plans in detail. Particularly, the biggest task was to address issues such as selection of the routes, ensuring efficient operation and passengers' safety and convenience. Location analytics and social media help Seoul Metropolitan Government (SMG) to realize the "Owl Bus" project and overcome these challenges.

The Problem

Since the subway line No. 1 opened in 1974 through to the transformation reform carried out in 2004, the Seoul Metropolitan SMG has steadily introduced measures to ensure greater convenience and better mobility of the citizens. However, students and workers such as sanitary workers or small business owners, who return home late night, found it hard to benefit from the preexisting systems. Most of them suffer from the poor working conditions and low salaries, yet they still had to pay the late-night extra charge when taking taxis to return home.

Second issue was the growing inconvenience due to late-night taxis" refusal of passengers and illegal operation. During late night and dawn hours, there are far less available taxis than people who are trying to hail a cab. Thus, illegal operations are prevalent by taxi drivers demanding extra fares, causing serious inconvenience to citizens. Additionally, there are practical limitations in controlling such irregularities. Firstly, there is a shortage of police officers responsible for preventing such violations, and even if the police catch an offender red-handed, it is difficult to obtain evidence to prove the driver's act of refusing passengers or demanding illegal excess fares.

Third issue was related to the public-private consensus on the need for new means of transportation to support urban dwellers" economic activities. Seoul, transformed into a global city within just 50 years, is emerging as a prime location of the global economy. As the city" industrial, economic and cultural activities expand in size and scope, the citizens reached a consensus on the need for a bus service that operates from midnight to dawn.

It was also considered that advanced nations such as Germany and the U.K. have already run such services to promote the safety of the citizens and their rights to mobility.

Private bus companies" selective operation on profitable routes was a long-running concern for SMG. Thus, it shifted from private to quasi-public bus operation system. In the new system, Seoul manages the bus routes and revenues while the private companies operate buses.

THE SOLUTION

Test Operation of Night Bus at the Request of the Citizens: Since 2012, the SMG has operated the 120 Dasan Call Center and the official blog to better listen to the voices of the citizens, and developed various policy measures based on the information collected through these channels. Along the way, an opinion was received that the late night taxi service is not only difficult to use but also imposes heavy financial burdens on users. An on-site survey conducted for about six months from October 2012 found it necessary to operate a late-night bus service. As a result, starting from April 19, 2013, the city government began operating two pilot routes exclusively for an after-midnight service.

Role of location analytics and social media: Social media and location analytics played a very important role in expanding the bus routes and selection of "Owl Bus" brand name. For three months following the launch of the test operation, the service was extremely well-received by 220,000 people, making it justifiable to raise the number of service routes. The seven new lines were determined by taking into consideration the heavy concentration of people on the move during late night hours. During the initial stages of mapping out how to operate the Seoul Night Bus, the issue of selecting bus routes emerged. The municipal government color-coded regions by call volume based on the location data provided by a private communication service provider, KT. Then, it analyzed the number of passengers who get on and off at each bus stop in the heavy-call volume regions and connected the dots to lead to the most pertinent routes. The data was used to construct a radial-shape network linking outer districts of the city with the hub areas such as Jongno and Gwanghwamun.

With news regarding the Late Bus spreading over SNS channels, citizens voluntarily suggested to name the late-night bus. Thus, the city government invited public ideas for the naming of the service and, as a result, the brand name "Owl Bus" and "N (Late Night)," and the character that portrays an owl operating a bus were selected. These symbols have been used to mark bus stop signs, bus route map and numbers and distinguish the late-night buses from ordinary ones. With the letter "N" in the bus number, the service began its full operation on September 16, 2014.

RESULTS

Real-time operation information: The service provides citizens with real-time operation information. Anyone who wants to take the "Owl Bus" can check the arrival time and location of the bus stop in advance through the website or smartphone apps. Meantime, given that the service operates late night, safety measures were critical to protect citizens. Besides the protective partition and speeding prevention device, it was made mandatory to inspect the vehicle before driving. The drivers with proven qualifications are also well remunerated so that they do not have to take on other vocational activities during the daytime hours and can fully concentrate during night time driving.

Safe and Affordable Means of Transportation for Citizens: The numbers of "Owl Bus" passengers are on the constant rise. A total of 1,735,000 people have taken the buses from September 2009 to June 2013, making the daily average passengers stand at around 7,000. As for economic aspects, passengers are expected to save approximately KRW 6,000 as the "Owl Bus" charges KRW 1,850 per trip while the average taxi fare in the same timeframe costs KRW 8,000. Given that the most of the passengers are students, self-employed small business owners or workers, the service is expected to help stabilize their household finances.

Meantime, most passengers are concentrated in the timeframe from midnight to 03:00, when students and workers return home completing their after-school self-study and night duties. As the unfrequented time tends to leave them more vulnerable, the "Owl Bus" is considered to help them move more safely. Notably, the "Safe returning-home service" provided in cooperation with the nearby police stations reinforce the safety.

Income redistribution for the economically disadvantaged: Before the operation of the "Owl Bus," one had to pay up to tens of thousands of won to move from the city center to a residential district outside the city. However, they now can complete their journey with just 1,850 won. As the savings will lead to higher disposable incomes, income redistribution effects are expected, too. As of 2013, the SMG estimates nearly KRW 14.1 billion worth of economic benefits have been redistributed.

Distribution of the manual for other local governments to benchmark: As residents of other cities express their interest in the "Owl Bus," through SNS channels, local governments and research institutes have inquired about the process in the run-up to the introduction and requested lectures on the "Owl Bus." With many metropolitan governments expressing their interest, the Busan Metropolitan Government has already begun operating the late night service by extending the operation hours of existing intracity buses and other cities such as Ulsan and Daejun consider introducing it, too.

RESOURCES

Budget: To finance the operation of the "Owl Bus," budget provision was needed to pay for the labor costs and the installation of safety facilities such as protective walls for drivers and a speeding prevention system. However, these expenses were covered by the joint management funds for the shift from private to quasi-public bus operation. Consequently, additional costs were not incurred.

Technology: Information systems connected inside the vehicles such as the Bus Management System, the Bus Information Unit and Bus Information Tool enable comprehensive control of the bus operations, and efficient adjustment of intervals while providing users and drivers with real time operation information.

Human resources: The "Owl Bus was introduced without incurring additional costs, and increased operation revenues too. The allocated resources are 45 vehicles and a total of 54 workers; 36 for driving and 18 for management.

Source: Bus Policy Department, the Seoul Metropolitan Government, South Korea.

TUTORIAL: MAPPING WITH GOOGLE FUSION TABLES

Google Fusion Tables is a web service to store, share, query, and visualize tabular business data overlaid on Google Maps. Tabular data can be visualized and shared in a variety of ways, including charts, maps, network graphs, or custom layout. California Sate, for example, shares government datasets using Fusion Tables (http://data.ca.gov/category/by-data-format/fusion-tables/) where the data can be viewed, filtered, and downloaded by citizens.

The data formats supported by **Fusion Tables** include spreadsheets, CSV files, and Keyhole Markup Language (KML, a file format used to display and map geographic data). Google also provides the Fusion Tables API (https://developers.google.com/fusiontables/) for managing data programmatically and an example library of Fusion Tables: https://sites.google.com/site/fusiontablestalks/stories.

In this tutorial, we will learn how to configure Fusion Tables to map and share your data online.

Getting Started with Fusion Tables

Step 1: Go to https://www.google.com/fusiontables/ and click on the "Create a Fusion Table" button. For this exercise, we will use Victoria, Australia's location of police stations data downloaded from http://data.gov.au/dataset/police-station-locations in the KML format (the data file and up-to-date tutorial is also available on the book companion website).

Step 2: Next, you will be asked to upload your data into the Fusion Table. To do so, you have four options:

1. Upload from your computer
2. Upload from Google Spreadsheets
3. Create an empty table (for manipulating data later)
4. Search other online publically available data

In this tutorial, we choose the "from this computer" and click "Browse File" to upload the data. Locate the data you want to open and click the "Next" button.

Step 3: Next, choose the format (i.e., comma separated, tab, colon, or other type) of data being uploaded (in this case KML). Leave the other options on their default settings and click the "Next" button.

Step 4: After the data is loaded, make sure that the correct row is selected for the column names (which is normally row 1) and click "Next."

Step 5: Once the data is imported, provide the following details and click "Finish."

Table—Provide a meaningful table name.

Allow export—If you check this, other users will be able to export your data into a CSV file.

Attribute data to—Here you can write a message that will be displayed when people view or use your data.

Attribution page link—Provide the attribution page URL or link, if any.

Description—Provide a meaningful description here that may help you remember what the data is about.

Step 6: Now your data is uploaded into the Fusion Table and you are ready to process, visualize, and share it.

Step 7: Fusion Tables auto-detect location data and display a tab called "Map of <location column name>." In this case, the "Map" tab is titled "Map of geometry." Click on "Map of geometry" to see a map of the police stations (Screenshot 18).

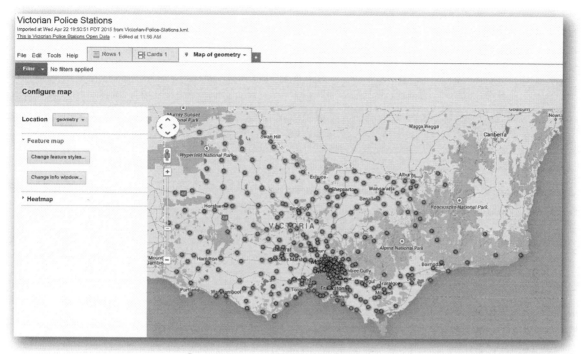

Screenshot 18. Map of police stations

If the Fusion Table does not automatically detect location information, then you need to configure it manually through the following steps:

1. Click on the "Rows" tab and find the column name that has the location data and click on the downward pointing arrow.
2. Next, click on "Change."
3. On the page that opens up, choose "Location" for the type and then click on the "Save" button.

Step 8: Next, double-click on a red place-mark to view more information about a police station.

Step 9: Once you've created a map, you can customize different aspects of it, including creating and customizing charts, creating custom cards, changing marker styles, and apply filters to your data.

Changing marker styles—To change the marker style (the red dots), use the following steps.

➢ Make sure that you are on the "Map" tab. Click "Tools→Change map→Change feature styles."

➢ Click on the "Marker" icon in the left panel and "Fixed" in the right panel.

➢ Choose a different marker style from the dropdown menu and click "Save."

➢ You can also assign different marker icons to different types of variables by using the "Bucket" option. For example, police stations in different regions can be marked with different icons.

Filtering data—Filters are variables from your table/data that will be used to filter out data for display. To apply filters to your data, use the following steps.

➢ Make sure that you are on the "Map" tab. Click on the "Filters" button available at the left upper side of the map.

➢ Select a filter that you want to apply from the dropdown list (e.g., we chose "Region").

After applying the filter, you will be offered all the distinct values for regions (in this case, four regions are displayed). We choose to display police stations from only one region (i.e., Northern Metro). Now only data about police stations from Northern Metro is displayed.

Customize the info window—the default information window that appears when you click on a red dot only uses the first ten columns from the data table, but you can customize which data appears and how it is displayed.

➢ Make sure that you are on the "Map" tab. Click on the "Tools→Change map," then click the "Change info window" button.

➢ Click on the checkboxes to add or remove information from the automatic info window template.

➢ You can also customize the overall style and content of the info window template by clicking the "Custom" tab. Once done, click on the "Save" button.

Adding charts—Fusion Tables lets you add charts to your data so that you compare and contrast multiple values at a glance.

➢ To add a chart, click on the red plus (+) sign and then click on "Add Chart" from the dropdown menu.

➤ Once a chart is added, you can choose different variables (e.g., continuous or categorical) to the chart depending on the type of chart you selected (e.g., pie chart, bar graph, line chart, or network chart). A chart type can be changed from the left panel.

➤ Once you selected the right type of chart, click on the "Done" button in the upper right-hand corner (Screenshot 19).

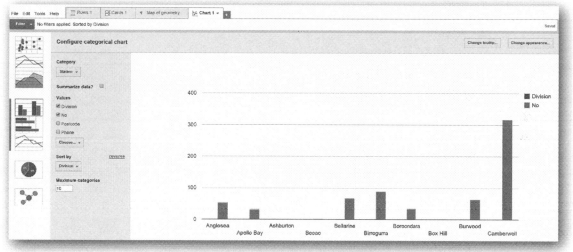

Screenshot 19. Configuring charts

Sharing your data—One of the main reasons you are using Fusion Tables is to make your data available for other to see and download. To share your map, use the following steps.

➤ Make sure that you are on the "Map" tab. Click on the "Tools" menu and then click on "Publish."

➤ You can either share it with a limited number of people through e-mail, or you can make it available over the Internet for everyone to see. In this exercise, we will make it available to the public.

➤ Click on the "Change" option under "Who has access." A new window will appear. Select the "public on the web" option and then click "Save."

➤ Next, you will be provided with a link and an HTML code for sharing your data. Copy it and click "Done." The code and the link can be embedded into your blog, website, or social media platforms. You can always get the link and code by clicking "Tools" and then "Publish."

➢ In a similar way, the charts you have created can be shared. Note that to share a chart, you must be at the "Chart" tab and then click "Tools→Publish." You will be provided with a code and link to share.

Review Questions

1. Define location analytics.
2. Explain the two main categories of location analytics.
3. What are the sources of location data.
4. What are the main applications of business data-driven location analytics?
5. What are the main applications of social media data-driven location analytics?
6. Discuss privacy concerns related to location analytics.

CHAPTER 9

SEARCH ENGINES ANALYTICS

SEARCH ENGINES are the gateways to social media and help users search for and find information. To be more precise, a search engine is an Internet service or software designed to search information on the web that corresponds to a request (e.g., keywords) specified by the user. Considering that there are billions of websites over the web, search engines play a crucial role in helping us find the right information in a limited amount of time. Before shifting our focus to search engines analytics, let's understand different types of search engines.

TYPES OF SEARCH ENGINES

Based on the mechanisms they operate, search engine can be divided into three types: 1) Crawler-based, 2) Directories, and 3) Metasearch engines.

CRAWLER-BASED

As the name suggests, crawler-based search engines create their databases or lists automatically, without any human intervention. Examples of crawler-based search engine are Google.com and Bing.com. Crawler-based search engines are widely used to find and access content over the Internet. They operate in three steps: 1) web crawling, 2) indexing, and 3) searching.

Web crawling—Search engines start by collecting and storing information about web pages. This mechanism is termed *web crawling*. A web crawler (also known as web spider or bot) is a computer program or software specifically designed to collect and store data about websites for indexing.

Indexing—Indexing helps classify a website correctly for searching purposes. The data crawled or extracted is then indexed and stored in a database for quick access. Every search engine may follow different techniques for indexing web page data. Common indexing techniques include storing meta tags (which are used in the header of a web page and provide descriptions of the website) and keywords related to a website.

Searching—Searching is the final step in search engine operations. When a user requests specific information by entering keywords in a search engine, the search engine queries the index and provides a list of the most relevant web pages by matching it with the indexed keywords. However, it may not be that simple; search engines use a variety of factors to rank and provide a list of matching websites.

A takeaway here is that in order to achieve good search results an organization must place keywords in section titles, images, and in the general content of its website. A keyword density of 5–8 percent (i.e., five to eight keywords per one hundred words) is an optimal number. Having important keywords embedded in a website enables a search engine robot to evaluate the website as being the most suitable site for the searched word. However, if one repeatedly uses the same keywords or definitions in page content, it may be perceived by a robot to be spamming (Yalçin and Köse 2010). Research has shown that the position of key words in a website, as well as their duplication, layout, and combination, impact web page visibility in a search engine, (Zhang and Dimitroff 2005) which can be improved by increasing the frequency of keywords in the title, the full text, and in both the title and full-text. In conjunction with key words, the overall design of a website is an important factor that must be taken into consideration when discussing search engine optimization. For example, flash animations, while aesthetically appealing, can negatively impact the SEO evaluation results because they cannot be indexed as easily by bots as more simply structured HTML content (Yalçin and Köse 2010). For a corporation to better understand its Internet presence, its website statistics should also be checked on a regular basis so as to understand both how users access and utilize the site and also what impact site changes may have on these behaviors.

DIRECTORIES

The listings in directories are manually compiled and created by human editors. People who want to be listed in a directory submit an address, title, and brief description of their website, which is then reviewed by the editor and included in it. Some good examples of human-created directories are Yahoo Directory, Open Directory, and LookSmart.

METASEARCH ENGINES

Metasearch engines compiles and display results from other search engines. When a user enters a query, the metasearch engine submits the query to several individual search engines, and results returned from all the search engines are integrated, ranked, and displayed to the user. Examples of meta–search engines include Metacrawler, Mamma, and Dogpile. By integrating results from several search engines, metasearch engines are capable of handling large amounts of data and can help us save time by focusing on one search engine.

Based on their scope, search engines can be divided into two types: 1) local and 2) global.

LOCAL SEARCH ENGINES

A search engine is local in the sense that it is embedded within a website and only indexes and searches the content of that website. Amazon's CloudSearch or any other search engine embedded within a website is an example of local search engine.

GLOBAL SEARCH ENGINES

Global search engines are used to search for content on the web. Google.com and Bing.com are examples of global search engines. However, note that global search engines can be localized. Google search, for example, can also embed within your website to help users find information on your website.

SEARCH ENGINE ANALYTICS

Generally, when we talk about search engine analytics, we mean two things,:1) search engine optimization and 2) search engine trend analysis.

SEARCH ENGINE OPTIMIZATION

Search engine optimization (SEO) are the techniques used to improve a website's ranking in a search engine result page (SERP) (Pan 2015). A SERP is the list of the results returned by a search engine in response to a user's query. SERPs generally have two types of results: organic and nonorganic search results. Organic results appear mainly because of their relevance to the user's query. Nonorganic search results include paid advertisements. A study tested the effect of sponsored ad ranks on the click-through and conversion rates for an online retailer and found that top positions usually had higher click through rates, but not necessarily higher conversion rates (Agarwal, Hosanagar et al. 2011).

Social media marketers strive to develop search engine strategies to make their websites appear at the top of search results. It is important for their websites to appear at top (e.g., in the top ten) in the SERP, as users pay closer attention to the top results on search engines (Pan, Hembrooke et al. 2007). The ranking becomes more crucial when the website is commercial by nature; that is, selling products or services. High rankings on SERPs can mean more Internet traffic to a website, which in some cases converts to more paying clients and higher return on investment (Weideman 2009).

For social media marketers, it is important to understand the mechanism behind the SERP ranking. There may be variety of factors search engines take into account to rank websites, such as keywords and relevance. However, the most important factor that determines SERP ranking is the PageRank. PageRank is a mechanism (or an algorithm, to be more precise) used by Google search engines to rank websites' SERPs. The websites that rank higher are displayed on the top of the search results page. Google's PageRank algorithm predominantly relies on the quality of incoming hyperlinks (or in-links) to rank websites. A website, for example, with in-links from a famous websites (e.g., cnn.com) will appear on the top of the SERP if compared with a website with no quality in-links or many low-quality in-links. To understand the in-link quality and number argument, consider Figure 12, where nodes represents web pages and lines represent in-links (arrowhead pointing to a page) and out-links (arrowhead pointing away from a page). The PageRank algorithm will place page B higher on the SERP, even though there are fewer in-links to B when compared to D. The reason for this ranking is that in-links to website B are from an important website; that is, A. Bottom line, your objective is to increase the number of quality in-links to your website.

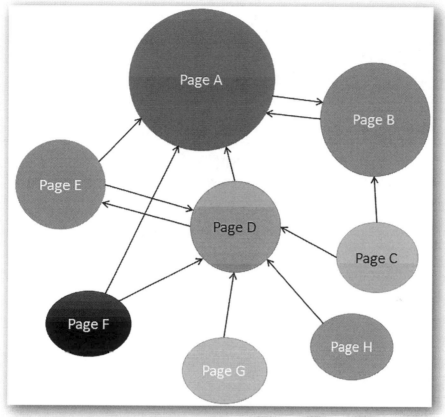

Figure 12. PageRank algorithm ranking example

By using, for example, Open SEO Stats (an extension for Google Chrome available at: http://pagerank.chromefans.org/), users can be determine the ranking of a website based on Google PageRank. Google PageRank uses a scale of 0 to 10, indicating the importance that the Google search engine allocates to the page. In addition to page ranking, Open SEO Stats also provides information about website traffic, hyperlink status, and speed of the page, among other things.

SEARCH TREND ANALYTICS

Search engine trends analytics deals with analyzing and understanding the keywords people use in a search engine. Search engine data are gateways into the minds of customers. Through search engines, customers search for what they want, thus search trend analysis can provide value information to the social marketers.

When it comes to trends analytics, Google Trends (http://www.google.com/trends/) is one of the most convenient and comprehensive search engine trend analysis tools. Google trends use massive amounts of search engine data to analyze the world's interests and predict trends. In the financial sector, Google Trends data, for example, has been used to detect "early warning signs" of stock market moves (Preis, Moat et al. 2013). In the health sector, Google Trends data has helped determine world flu epidemics (Ginsberg, Mohebbi et al. 2009). Engineers at Google.org, for instance, using Google Trends data, found a strong correlation among the searches for flu-related topics and the numbers of actual flu cases circulating in different countries and regions around the world (Ginsberg, Mohebbi et al. 2009).

In this chapter, we use Google Trends for search engine analytics. From a business perspective, Google Trends can help also answer a variety of questions, including the following.

- How people search for your brand?
- When does interest spike in your products or services?
- Which keywords drive more traffic?
- Which regions are interested in your brand?
- What are trending topics over the Internet?
- How are your competitors performing?

Search Engine Analytics Tools

Google Trends: Google Trends (http://trends.google.com/) is a search engine analytics tool. This chapter includes a detailed tutorial on Google Trends.

Canopy: Canopy is multimedia analytics tool designed to support deep investigation of large multimedia collections, such as images, videos, and documents. More information on Canopy is available here: http://www.vacommunity.org/article32

Google Alerts: Google Alerts (https://www.google.com/alerts) is a content detection and notification service that automatically notifies users when new content over the Internet (e.g., social media, web, blogs, video and/or discussion groups) matches a set of search terms based on user queries. Users are alerted through e-mail. Find out about how to use Google Alerts.

Icerocket: Icerocket (http://www.icerocket.com/) specializes in blog searches and also captures activity on Facebook, Twitter, and Flickr.

Social Mention: Social Mention (http://socialmention.com/) is similar to Google Alerts, but it only focuses on social media sites, and you can choose to focus on particular areas, such as blogs. With Social Mention you can monitor for the appearance of particular keywords and it will give you information on related users, hashtags, and more.

TweetBeep: TweetBeep (http://tweetbeep.com/) is like Google Alerts for Twitter. Choose some keywords and receive daily search results via e-mail.

TUTORIAL: SEARCH ENGINE ANALYTICS WITH GOOGLE TRENDS

Google Trends uses percentages to analyze trend results. For example, if someone searches for the term *analytics* in Australia in June of 2015, Google Trends analyzes and displays the percentage of all searches for the keyword *analytics* in June in Australia.

TYPES OF ANALYTICS PROVIDED BY GOOGLE TRENDS

In its current form, Google Trends provides six types of analytics available at the drop-down box at the left upper corner. They are as follows.

- ✓ Year in Search
- ✓ Trending Searches
- ✓ Trending on YouTube
- ✓ Top Charts
- ✓ Explore
- ✓ Subscription

Among them, the "Explore" option is the most important from the search engine analytics perspective and we will look it in detail in this chapter. But, first let's briefly discuss the other analytic reports.

YEAR IN SEARCH

Year in Search is a short commercial video clip (with accompanying details that can be further explored) that summarizes the world's most popular searches in a particular year. Currently, a year in search video is available for the year 2014.

Trending Searches

Trending Searches provides a list of top-ten searches on a daily basis for a specific country. The search results for particular data are updated regularly.

Trending on YouTube

Like Trending Searches, Trending on YouTube provides a list of top-ten videos on a daily basis for a specific country. The search results for particular data are updated regularly.

Top Charts

Top Charts displays a list of trending real-world people, places, and things ranked in order of search interest in a particular year. With Top Charts, for example, one can see a list of the top-ten most searched athletes, consumer electronics, YouTube videos, topics, and global news, among other things. Top Charts depends on Knowledge Graph technology to provide the rankings (Knowledge Graph is Google's knowledge base that understands facts about real-world things (e.g., people, places and things) and their connections. Knowledge Graph is used to enhance users' search experiences by providing them structured and detailed information about the topic they are searching for. More information on Knowledge Graph can be found here: http://www.google.co.kr/insidesearch/features/search/knowledge.html). The charts can be customized to show either global search trends or search trends in a particular country. Historical search trends going back to the year 2001 are available.

Explore

The Explore option is a very important resource in search engine analytics. The Explore option lets you analyze search engine trends related one or more search terms across time and location. Recall some of the questions we mentioned earlier, such as, "How do people search for your brand?" "When does interest spike in your products or services?" "Which keywords drive more traffic?" "Which regions are interested in your brand?" The Explore option can help you answer these questions. Here is how to start using the Explore option.

Step 1: Open Google Trends: http://www.google.com/trends/.

Step 2: Click on the "Trends" option in the upper left-hand corner. Next, from the dropdown menu, select "Explore."

Step 3: Next, click on "Add Terms" to enter the search terms for what you want to analyze. Repeat this process until you have entered all the desired terms. In this case, we entered three terms: "iPhone 4," "Galaxy S4," and "LG Optimus." The results are grouped into three categories: 1) interests over time, 2) regional interests, and 3) related searches. Below, we discuss each of the categories in detail.

INTERESTS OVER TIME

Interests over time (in terms of number of searches) are displayed in the form of a graph below the terms showing their popularity over time (Screenshot 22). The numbers on the graph reflect how many searches have been done for the terms, relative to the total number of searches done on Google over time. Note that the numbers represent search volume relative to the highest point on the graph, which is always 100. The data on the search volume is normalized and presented on a scale from 0–100, thus it does not represent absolute search volume numbers.

You can examine different points on the graph by hovering your mouse over them. The graph also display news headlines (if available) related to the terms. The news headlines are indicated by capital letters displayed over the lines and correspond to the year of the news. By hovering your cursor over the letters, you will be able to see the detailed news. You can also see the forecasted results by checking the "Forecast" checkbox in the upper right-hand corner of the graph (forecasts are always available). You can also notice bars appearing next to the chart. The bar height represents the average of all data points on the graph for that search term.

From the graph it is clear that interest in smartphones corresponds to their launch dates, and that interest is much stronger in the first couple of months and then declines.

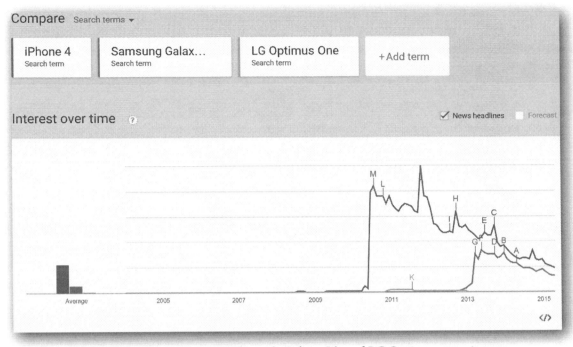

Screenshot 20. Interest in iPhone 4, Galaxy S4, and LG Optimus over time

REGIONAL INTERESTS

The "Regional Interests" section shows interest in the search terms with respect to geography (Screenshot 20). Note that for each search term, regional interest is shown in a separate window. In the screenshot below, we are looking at the regional interest in the "iPhone 4" term. You can choose the "Galaxy S4" term by clicking over it. You can also switch between region and city view by the clicking the appropriate option in the top right-hand corner. From the results it is clear that top cities interested in the iPhone 4 are Ho Chi Minh City, Hanoi, Bangkok, London, Singapore, and Manila.

Screenshot 21. Regional interest in iPhone 4s

However, interest in the Galaxy S4 is coming from Jakarta, Istanbul, Sydney, Bucharest, Berlin, Munich, and Vienna (Screenshot 21). You can see the detailed regional search volume by clicking on a region of interest.

Screenshot 22. Regional interest in Galaxy S4

RELATED SEARCHES

The "Related Searches" section (available near the bottom of the page) shows the popular search terms similar to your search terms. Using this function, for example, you can find which topics will potentially drive more traffic, "smartphone" or "Galaxy S4"? Knowing trending topics related to our products/services can help us optimize a campaign.

Now that you understood the basic of Google Trends, let's focus on how to use the research function more effectively.

UNDERSTANDING THE RESEARCH FUNCTION

Using Search Operators

You can use search operators to filter the types of results that you see in Trends. Use the Table 3 to learn about executing your search correctly.

Table 3. Executing your research correctly

Search Terms	The Results Displayed
Social media analytics	Results can include searches containing the terms "social," "media," and "analytics" in any order.
"Social media analytics"	Results will only include the exact search terms included inside of the quotation marks.
social + analytics	Results can include searches containing the words "social" OR "analytics."
social – analytics	Results will include searches containing the word "social," but will exclude searches containing the word "analytics."

Note that Google Trends searches ignore special characters (such as apostrophes, single quotes, and parentheses). Similarly, misspelled words and spelling variations are considered as separate words. For example, the term "analytic" and "analytics" will be considered two separate words.

Grouping Search Terms

Overall, you can search up to five groupings at one time, with up to twenty-five search terms in each grouping. Consider the following example.

- ✓ iPhone 2 + Galaxy S2 + LG G (Grouping 1)
- ✓ iPhone 3 + Galaxy S3 + LG Optimus F3 (Grouping 2)
- ✓ iPhone 4 + Galaxy S4 (Grouping 3)
- ✓ iPhone 5 + Galaxy S5 + LG Optimus F6 (Grouping 4)
- ✓ iPhone 6+ Galaxy S6 (Grouping 5)

Customizing the Search

From the dropdown menu available at the top of the page, search results can be customized with respect to countries, years, categories (such as business or games), and types of web resources to focus on (such as web search, image search, news search, Google shopping, and YouTube search). You can also select custom data from the date dropdown menu by clicking on the "Select Data" option. For example, in the example above, we restricted our search to January 2010–April 2015. Note that currently, trend data is only available from 2004 onward.

Review Questions

1. What is the function of a search engine?
2. Explain different types of search engines.
3. Differentiate between local and global search engines.
4. What is search engine analytics?
5. Explain the two main categories of search engine analytics.
6. What is the purpose of search engine optimization?
7. What is the purpose of search engine trend analysis?

CHAPTER 10

ANALYTICS–BUSINESS ALIGNMENT

It is simply not enough to have a social media analytics tool ready to mine data. Analytics should be strategically aligned to support existing business goals. Without a well-crafted and aligned social media strategy, your business will struggle to get the desired outcomes from analytics. This chapter introduces social media analytics and business alignment concepts, social media alignment matrices, the role of the chief information officer (CIO) in facilitating the alignment, and the steps needed to formulate a social media strategy.

UNDERSTANDING SOCIAL MEDIA AND BUSINESS ALIGNMENT

As with any other technology, aligning social media objectives and goals with the objectives of the organization should be the starting point of any social media analytics initiative. The alignment of social media analytics with business objectives can be seen as analogous to the famous Chinese Yin and Yang philosophy, where two seemingly opposing forces (in this case, social media and business) complement and reinforce each other (Figure 13).

Figure 13. Aligning Social Media Analytics with business goals (Yin and Yang philosophy)

Figure 14 provides example scenarios for aligning social media with business objectives. If the business goal is to understand customer sentiments expressed over social media, the social media analytics should be designed to facilitate this objective. It may require, for example, tools and skills for extracting and analyzing tweets or comments posted on a Facebook fan page. Or, for example, if your business objective is to identify influential social media customers and their position in the network, your focus should be on social media networks.

Example Business Question	Layers of Interest	Data Source	Example of Tools
Is the social media conversation about our company, product, or service positive, negative, or neutral?	Text Analytics	Tweets Comments Blog posts Reviews	Discovertext Lexalytics Semanteria
Which content posted over social media is resonating more with my customers?	Actions Analytics	Likes Shares Views Mentions	Google Analytics Hootsuite
Who are our influential social media nodes, and what is their position in the network?	Network Analytics	Fan network Follower network	NodeXL Flocker Netlytic Mentionmapp
How is our mobile app performing?	Mobile Analytics	Total sessions New users Time spent	Countly Mixpanel Google Mobile Analytics
Where are our social media customers located?	Location Analytics	Geo-map IP address GPS	Google Fusion Table Tweepsmap Followerwonk
Which social media platforms are driving most traffic to our corporate website?	Hyperlink Analytics	Hyperlinks In-links Co-links	Webometrics Analyst VOSON
Which keywords and terms are trending?	Research Engine Analytics	Trending topics	Google Trends

Figure 14. Aligning analytics with business objectives

SOCIAL MEDIA ANALYTICS ALIGNMENT MATRIX

The extent and breadth of your social media analytics alignment with business goals will be determined by a variety of factors, including the availability of technical, financial, administrative, and leadership resources, and its potential to achieve business goals. Aligning information technologies with business objectives has been widely studied field (Henderson and Venkatraman 1993). Aligning social media analytics with business objectives may require a comprehensive approach like the strategic alignment model suggested by Henderson and Venkatraman (1993). In this book, we use a simplified social media analytics alignment matrix provided in Figure 15. On the Y axis of the matrix is "resource availability," which refers to the availability of financial, technical, administrative, and leadership resources for social media analytics. On the X axis of the matrix is the impact of social media analytics alignment in terms of its potential to achieve business goals (or its potential to generate economic value and return on investment). Depending on the two variables (i.e., resources availability and its potential), your social media analytics alignment with business goals can fall into four possible quadrants. Your alignment resides in the "highly aligned" quadrant, for example, when leadership, financial, administrative, and technical resources are available to leverage and (sustain) social media analytics and its potential is high in terms of achieving business goals. For instance, mining the seven layers of social media data is technically and financially demanding, but rewarding in terms of the creation of economic value to the firm. And your social media analytics alignment efforts reside in the "not aligned" quadrant when its potential to achieve business goals and your resource availability is low.

Generally, your social media analytics efforts should focus on highly aligned and high-impact alternatives. Nevertheless, your business goals and availability of resources will play an important role in determining the depth of your analytical efforts and resulting quadrant on the matrix. For instance, using Facebook's built-in analytical tools is financially and technically less challenging (and hence less rewarding) when compared to owning a sophisticated analytical tool, which may require technical and financial resources but will be highly rewarding in terms of achieving business goals.

The social media analytics alignment matrix will guide us throughout the social media strategy formulation process. The alignment matrix is flexible. One can replace the variables at both the axes with any other variables of interest. For example, we can place criticality of social media analytics (the extent to which the analytics is critical to the business) on the Y axis and sensitivity of the analytics (e.g., in terms of security, privacy, or ethics) on X axis and determine the extent of your alignment. Your social media analytics alignment, for instance, will be considered "highly aligned" if it is business critical, but less sensitive.

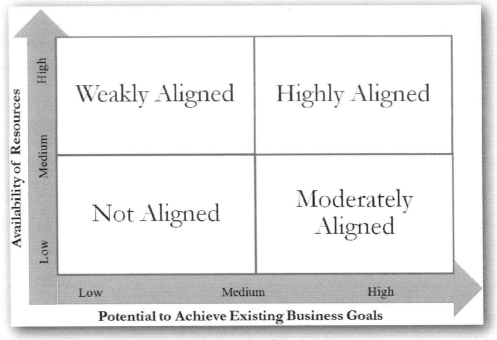

Figure 15. Social Media Alignment Matrix

ROLE OF CIO AND IT MANAGEMENT

Senior IT executives, particularly the CIO, play an important role in envisioning and creating aligned social media analytics strategy. The CIO is the person in charge of managing and aligning information communications technologies (ICTs) to achieve business-wide goals. The role of CIO has evolved from a technical guru to an informed leader, communicator, and strategic thinker. For a sustained strategic IT–business goals alignment, a CIO should possess the following skills and competences (Dawes 2008).

Strategic Thinking and Evaluation

- ✓ Business and policy reasoning
- ✓ IT investment for value creation
- ✓ Performance assessment
- ✓ Evaluation and adjustment

Systems Orientation

- ✓ Environmental awareness
- ✓ System and social dynamics
- ✓ Stakeholders and users
- ✓ Business processes
- ✓ Information flow and workflow

Appreciation for Complexity

- ✓ Communication
- ✓ Negotiation
- ✓ Cross-boundary relationships
- ✓ Risk assessment and management
- ✓ Problem solving

Information Stewardship

- ✓ Information policies
- ✓ Data management
- ✓ Data quality
- ✓ Information sharing and integration
- ✓ Records management
- ✓ Information preservation

Technical Leadership

- ✓ Communication and education
- ✓ Architecture
- ✓ Infrastructure
- ✓ Information and systems security
- ✓ Support and services
- ✓ IT workforce investments

FORMULATING A SOCIAL MEDIA STRATEGY

Formulating a social media strategy is not much different than overall information technology (IT) strategy of an organization. The purpose of formulating social media strategy is to create rules and procedures to align your social media engagement with business goals. Planning an aligned social media strategy should follow a strategy formulation process similar to that used by IT management as suggested by Luftman et al. (2004), though some additional steps are needed to account for the unique nature of social media technologies.

STEPS IN FORMULATING A SOCIAL MEDIA STRATEGY

The following steps will lead to the formulation of a sound social media strategy.

Get Hold of an Executive Champion

For any organizational strategy formulation and implementation, the sponsorship of a senior-level executive is crucial. The most important factor for success in social media analytics is not technology, but leadership and top management commitment. Success is possible only when the transformation is steered through strong leadership: setting direction, building momentum, and ensuring the disciplined execution of an inspiring vision and ambitious plans. A social media executive champion will be someone with charisma and the power to enforce social media strategy in the agency. It usually is the head of the department or the government chief information officer (GCIO). Enlisting the support of a champion is crucial for your social media efforts to be fruitful. A champion should have several attributes including, power, vision, resources, and willingness to sacrifice, and persistence to support the change (Luftman, Bullen et al. 2004).

Build a Cross-Functional Team

The first step in formulating a social media strategy is to create a cross-functional team with senior management members from all the departments, including the IT department. Ideally, this team should be led by a CIO. Having a cross-functional team will make sure that all the stakeholders have their say and have the ownership of the social media analytics initiative.

ASSESS YOUR ORGANIZATIONAL CULTURE

Understanding organization's vision, values, norms, systems, assumptions, and beliefs about social media is very crucial. Is your organization ready to embrace social media analytics? What are the organization's assumptions and beliefs about social media analytics? Embracing social media in all aspect of business will require organizational cultural transformation at all levels. In order to implement strategic initiatives that will change how the organization thinks about social media, it is important to understand the current status of the organizational culture. Understanding an organizational culture and transforming it is a very complex task and is beyond the scope of this book. A round table with the team members may provide some clues on the organization's social media readiness. In addition, a variety of organizational culture assessment and change tools are available on the market that can be used to access and highlight the need for a culture change. For example, The Organizational Culture Assessment Instrument (OCAI) is free tool for diagnosing organizational culture (developed by professors Robert Quinn and Kim Cameron) and Culture Builder Toolkit developed by Corporate Culture Pros. The bottom line is that with the cultural assessment, you want to make sure that your organization is ready to embrace social media and that it has the necessary vision and will to leverage it.

REVIEW YOUR CURRENT SOCIAL MEDIA PRESENCE

Before formulating a social media strategy, you need to document your current social media use and presence. You may start by asking the team members about their current social media status and by conducting a search for social media pages representing your organization. The best way to do it would be to arrange small, interactive seminars. Your objective is find out all the officially sanctioned and unauthorized social media outlets, including blogs, wikis, fan pages, and Twitter pages that use your organization's name. For example, you may use topsy.com to search for social media profiles representing your organization. You can also employ a SWOT (Strength, Weakness, Opportunities, and Threats) analysis to determine your current social media landscape. Documenting your current status will help you streamline your social media presence. This activity will become a basis for your organizational "as-is" state and for understanding your current social media use and strategic positioning.

Determine Your Objectives

Having understood the current stage of your social media presence, the next step will be to create a list of the objectives and goals that you want to achieve through your social media presence. With a clear idea of what you want to accomplish with social media, you are likely to put together a sound social media strategy. Clearly defining your goals and objectives is important, as different social media goals require different sets of actions and tools. Below are some commonly identified objectives by governments.

- ➤ To share news, alerts, and updates through mainstream social media platforms, including Twitter, Facebook, and YouTube.
- ➤ To implement a participatory platform (e.g., blog) where customers can submit ideas and suggestions and providing them the opportunity to participate in business strategy making.
- ➤ To increase awareness about products/services by disseminating information on social media platforms.
- ➤ To attract customers by driving traffic from social media platforms to corporate websites.
- ➤ To network and engage in dialogue with customers.

Each department may have different goals and objectives to be achieved through social media, so creating a broader social media policy will make sure each department has its say. The social media engagement matrix introduced earlier can be used here to determine the ease of achieving an objective against it impact.

Aligning Social Media Goals with Business Goals

At mentioned earlier, aligning social media goals with business goals is vital. In addition to each goal being specific, realistic, and measurable, it should be aligned with the existing business goals and strategy. If the organizational goal is to network with customers via social media platforms, the social media strategy should be designed to facilitate this objective.

Develop Your Content Strategy

Establishing a social media presence is the easy part; sustaining it is the real challenge. Developing a sound content strategy will make sure you know what to post, when to post, and how to post. Content strategy is tied to your goals and only the content that supports your goals should be developed and posted. A sound content strategy should at minimum answer the following questions.

- ✓ What type of content should we post to social media; for example, news, updates, alerts?
- ✓ How often should we post the content? Daily or weekly?
- ✓ Who will create the content?
- ✓ Is the content approved by the organization?
- ✓ Who will respond to follow-up suggestions and comments?
- ✓ How will the feedback be handled? etc.

PLATFORM STRATEGY

Platform strategy should detail the type of social media platform utilized to achieve your objectives. Your platform selection decision is tied to your business goals and objectives. If your aim is to share news, alerts, and updates, you may choose existing mainstream social media platforms, such as Twitter, Facebook, and YouTube. However, if you are looking for a platform to crowd-source ideas, a purpose-built Web 2.0 platform may be needed. This will also determine what type of resources you need, as discussed next.

RESOURCE CONSIDERATIONS

It is crucial to understand your desired level of social media engagement, as it will determine the type of resources (technical, human, and financial) you will need to pursue the goals. For example, if your goal is to establish an idea-generation platform to solicit creative ideas, in-house, purpose-built platform may be needed. Bear in mind that establishing and sustaining even a simple Facebook fan page needs considerable planning and human, financial, and technical resources. For example, it requires regular updates, answers to customer complaints and comments, and extraction and analysis of the data (e.g., tweets or comments) for better decision making.

ESTABLISH A SOCIAL MEDIA OWNERSHIP PLAN AND POLICY

A social media ownership plan and policy should outline the relative rights and responsibilities of employers and employees. Ownership plans covers social media ownership in terms of both accounts and activities such as accounts themselves, individual and pages profiles, platform content, and posting activity. Policies related to social media clarify issues related to personal and professional use, trade secrets, intellectual property, confidentiality, etc. Courtney Hunt (2014) has done a great job of providing social media ownership guidelines. The guidelines touch on the following areas related to social media ownership (Hunt 2014).

Agency accounts and profiles—This part of the ownership plan deals with all the social media accounts and activities, such as accounts themselves, individual and page profiles, platform content, and posting activity. Ideally, all the agency social media profiles should be owned the agency.

Individual profiles—Employees' social media profiles are owned by the individuals, but for the sake of agency reputation, governments should provide all employees with guidelines about how they should represent themselves on social media.

Contact information—Social media allows people to have multiple contact addresses (e.g., e-mail), and this policy should specify which contact the employee should display on their personal profile. A good practice is that employees include both a personal and a professional address.

Contacts—This policy should specify the rules for social media contacts made during the employment period (e.g., through LinkedIn). For example, you might specify that the contacts made are joint property, but that employees can keep their contacts after leaving the organization. However, organizations should have an internal system or mechanism to capture the important contacts.

Comments—Ownership strategy should also provide policies and guidelines on whether and how employees can comment on a variety of social media platforms. For example, when commenting, employees should make it clear whether they are commenting on behalf of the agency or expressing their personal thoughts.

Posting—What should and should not be posted to the social media platform is covered here. Clearly defining posting rules can help avoid issues with trade secrets, intellectual property, confidentiality, defamation, etc.

Groups—Organizations may establish policies and guidelines about the kind of groups employees can join or be members of. Allowing employees to join groups that promote your business goals is encouraged.

Privacy settings—By setting guidelines for social media privacy settings, agencies may encourage employees to set their social media privacy settings in the best interest of the both individuals and the agency.

This paper (http://www.socialfish.org/wp-content/downloads/socialfish-policies-whitepaper.pdf) gives further useful guidelines on the structure and characteristics of a sound social media policy.

SELECT SUCCESS METRICS

Success metrics will help you evaluate your social media strategy's effectiveness. Clearly defined metrics should be in place to measure the success of social media use in your organization. Metrics will help you determine whether social media actually is making a difference in your business. Depending on the type of social media engagement, success metrics may vary. For example, if the prime objective of your social media use is to engage customers in dialogue, the number of comments may be used as a metric. Or if it is to promote awareness, then the number of likes, shares, and page views may provide some indicators.

USE ANALYTICS TO TRACK PROGRESS

Social media analytics should be used evaluate your social media presence and to see how your organization is performing. For example, Google Analytics (discussed in the previous chapter) can provide a variety of analytical measures. Hootsuite Pro also offers advanced analytics and reporting for your social media measurement needs. The important thing to note is that your analytical tools should be configured to match your success metrics and business goals.

SOCIAL MEDIA STRATEGY IMPLEMENTATION PLAN

Information technology strategies are crafted carefully, but implemented rarely. A strategy implementation plan is an essential part of the social media strategy formulation process. This plan plans outlines strategies and tactics to put the strategic plans into action. The strategy implementation process can vary from organization to organization and depend on a variety of factors including support from senior executives and involvement of members from key departments. Four major barriers to strategic implantation are (Kaplan and Norton 2001):

> ➢ 85 percent of executive teams spend less than one hour per month discussing strategy.
> ➢ 60 percent don't link budgets to strategy.

> Only 25 percent of managers have incentives linked to strategy.
> Only 5 percent of the workforce understands the strategy.

The best way to go is to select team members from key departments who understand the purpose of the plan and the steps involved in implementing it. Establish a mechanism to regularly discuss progress reports and let team members know what has been accomplished. Communicate the plan throughout the agency and clearly specify ownerships, deadlines, and accountabilities.

Periodic Review

In the face of rapid technological, business, and social changes, the social media strategy should be periodically reviewed. The review will make sure that the initial assumption made about the external and internal factors (e.g., technology, vision, budgets) are still relevant.

Managing Social Media Risks

Engaging through social media introduces new challenges related to privacy, security, data management, accessibility, social inclusion, governance, and other information security issues. Risk, in simple words, is the possibility of losing something of value such as, intellectual or physical capital. A comprehensive definition of risk is provided by National Institute of Standards and Technology (NIST), which states that "risk is a function of the likelihood of a given threat-source's exercising a particular potential vulnerability, and the resulting impact of that adverse event on the organization." Here we will focus on the risk arising from social media use and define it as the potential of losing something of value (such as information, reputation, or goodwill) due to the use of social media tools and technologies.

Social media–related risks needs to be managed properly, both from the strategic and technological points of view. To minimize the damage, organizations need proactive, rather than reactive, social media risk-management strategy. A simple but effective way to proactively manage social media risks is through the social media crisis management loop (Figure 15), which includes four iterative steps: 1) identify, 2) access, 3) mitigate, and 4) evaluate. In the identification stage, potential risks are identified, which, in the assessment stage, are assessed and prioritized in terms of probability of occurrence and impact on the agency. In the mitigation stage, risk mitigation strategies are formulated and implemented. Finally, periodic assessment and reviews are carried out in the evaluation stage of the risk-management loop. Below, we discuss each step in detail.

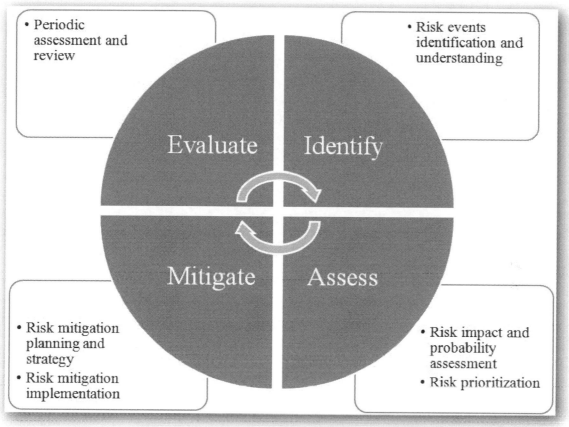

Figure 16. Social Media Risk-management Framework

RISK IDENTIFICATION

Risk identification is the process of identifying social media threats in terms of vulnerabilities and exploits that could potentially inhibit your organization from achieving its objectives. At this stage, your goal is to identify potential accidental or malicious risks that can come from within or outside the company. Examples of social media–related security breaches are hacking, information leaks, phishing, and impersonation. Phishing and hacking are examples of malicious outsider attacks. Famous social media platforms (such as Facebook, Twitter, and YouTube) are riskier than less famous ones (Webber 2012). According a study based on surveys and interviews with ninety-nine professionals and thirty-six companies (Webber 2012), the main social media risks identified were 1) damage to reputation, 2) release of confidential information, 3) legal, regulatory, and compliance violations, 4) identity theft and hijacking, and 5) loss of intellectual property. Other potential social media risks include malware, loss of privacy, and social engineering attacks.

RISK ASSESSMENT

Risk assessment is "the process of assessing the probabilities and consequences of risk events if they are realized" (MITRE 2014). The risk assessment process determines the likelihood of a social media risk event that could impact the organization economically, technically, politically, and socially. The potential risks identified in the earlier step are priorities and ranked based on probability of occurrence and impact on an organization (Garvey 2008).

Probability (P) is the likelihood of occurrence of a risk event and can take a value from 0 to 1. Probability can, for example, be assigned to risks events as follows.

Certain to occur (P=1)—The risks with a P value equal to 1 are the risks that will certainly happen. In other words, they have a 100 percent chance of occurring.

Extremely sure to occur (P=> 95 <1)—The risks, for example, with a probability value greater than 0.95 and less than 1.0 can be considered as "extremely sure to happen" risks. In other words, they have a 95–100 percent chance of occurring.

Almost sure to occur (P= > 0.85 <= 0.95)—The risks with a probability value greater than 0.85 and less than or equal to 0.95 can be considered as "very likely to occur" risks. The can be said to have an 85–95 percent chance of occurring.

Very likely to occur (P=> 0.75 <=0.85)—These are the risks with a 75–85 percent chance of occurring.

Likely to occur (P=> 0.65 <=0.75)—these are the risks with a 65 to 75 percent chance of occurring.

Slightly likely to occur (P=> 0.55 <=0.65)—these are the risks with a 65 to 75 percent chance of occurring.

Evenly likely to occur (P=> 0.45 <=0.55)—these are the risks with a 45 to 55 percent chance of occurring.

Impact of a risk event can be characterized as 1) severe, 2) significant, 3) moderate, 4) minor, or 5) minimal. A risk event is considered severe, for example, if it has devastating economical, technological, political, or social impact on your agency. And a risk is considered minimal if its impact is very low or negligible.

Based on the impact and probability, social media risks can be prioritized as 1) high, 2) medium, or 3) low (Table 5).

High priority risks—The risks that, if they happen, will have severe economic, technological, political, or social impact on your agency. These are the risks that needs immediate attention and should be managed carefully.

Medium priority risks—The medium-probability risks that, if they happen, will have considerable economic, technological, political, or social impact on your agency.

Low priority risks—The low probability risks that, if they happen, will have low economic, technological, political, or social impact on your agency.

As shown in the Figure 16, you can assign other probabilities in a similar way.

Probability (P)	Chance of occurrence	Priority
P=1	Certain to occur	High Priority Risks
P=> 0.95 <1	Extremely sure to occur	High Priority Risks
P=> 0.85 <= 0.95	Almost sure to occur	High Priority Risks
P=> 0.75 <=0.85	Very likely to occur	High Priority Risks
P=> 0.65 <=0.75	Likely to occur	High Priority Risks
P=> 0.55 <=0.65	Slightly likely to occur	Medium Priority Risks
P=> 0.45 <=0.55	Evenly likely to occur	Medium Priority Risks
P=> 0.35 <=0.45	Less than an even chance	Medium Priority Risks
P=> 0.25 <=0.35	Less likely to occur	Low Priority Risks
P=> 0.15 <=0.25	Not likely to occur	Low Priority Risks
P=> 0.00 <=0.15	Certainly sure not to occur	Low Priority Risks

Figure 17. Risk probability and prioritization assessment

RISK MITIGATION

The risks prioritized and ranked in the earlier stage should be physically, technically, and procedurally managed, eliminated, or reduced to an acceptable level. Dependent on the nature of the risks, different strategies should be used; for example, accidental risks posed by employees (e.g., posting copyright material online or tweeting some confidential information) can be eliminated by training, awareness programs, and by having sound social media policy in place. Hacking attacks, for example, can be mitigated using updated antivirus systems and by creating an extra layer of security, such as a two-mode authentication technique (discussed later). Typical risks mitigation strategies are:

Risks management governance—New governance structures, roles, and policies should be created within your business for properly managing social media risks. These activities may involve identifying and empowering a social media risk-management manager, developing a business-wide risk-management strategy, identifying actions and steps needed to implement the strategy, and determining the resources required to mitigate the risks (Garvey 2008). Create a social media risk-management governance structure by involving all key departments, including IT, finance, public relations, human resources, legal, and communications. All of these components play an important role in identifying and mitigating social media risks.

Training and awareness—Provide education and spreading awareness on legal issues such as copyright, intellectual property, defamation, slander, and anti-trust issues.

Social media policy—Create a sound social media policy that outlines the relative rights and responsibilities of employers and employees.

Secure your social media platforms—Secure your social media platforms to minimize the impact or likelihood of the risk.

The following are some techniques you can use to secure your social media platforms.

Use strong passwords—to protect your social media accounts (Twitter, Facebook, YouTube, blogs, etc.) always use strong passwords. A password is considered strong when it:

- ✓ Is at least ten characters long.
- ✓ Has a combination of uppercase and lowercase letters, numbers, and symbols.
- ✓ Does not include your personal information such as phone numbers, birthdays, name, etc.
- ✓ Does not use common words such as "mypassword," "ilikeyou," etc.
- ✓ Does not use alphabetical sequences (such as "abcd1234") or keyboard sequences (such as "qwerty")
- ✓ Is not reused across websites; that is, your Twitter account password should be unique to Twitter.
- ✓ Is memorized or kept in a safe place if written.

Securing Your Facebook Account

Two-mode authentication—Facebook's two-mode authentication (or login approval, as Facebook calls it) is a great way to secure your account. It provides an extra layer of security that uses your phone to protect your account. For example, if your account is compromised or someone figures out your password, they will still not be able to access to your account unless they have physical access to your phone. Each time you login in from an unknown browser or computer, you will need to provide a security code to access your account (unless you list the device as secure). The security code is only provided to you through your phone via a text message or through a third-party code g application installed on your smartphone, such as the Google Authenticator application.

> ➤ *Steps*: Login to your Facebook account → Go to "Account Settings" → "Security Settings" → "Login Approvals" → "Get Started."

Clicking on the "Get Started" button will take you through a step-by-step process to enable the two-mode authentication. Note that the codes cannot be texted to a landline or Google Voice, so you will need a mobile phone to configure the authentication properly.

Trusted contact—The trusted contact is an account recovery feature provided by Facebook to help you access your account securely through your friends if you have trouble accessing your account. You can select three to five friends to be your trusted contacts who can be reached through means other than Facebook (e.g., phone or e-mail). In case of emergency, you can contact your trusted contacts and Facebook will provide each of them a security code for you with instructions on how to help you. You can then use the codes to recover your Facebook account.

> ➤ *Steps:* Login to your account → "Account Settings" → "Security Settings" → "Trusted Contacts" → "Choose Trusted Contacts."

Review your login history—It is a good practice to regularly review your account login history and location.

> ➤ *Steps:* Login to your account → "Account Settings" → "Security Settings" → "Where you're Logged In."

Your location is estimated with your public IP (Internet protocol) or address. Bringing your cursor over the location will display the IP used to access the account. Make sure the IP address is associated with the organization. The page will also provide information about other devices used to access the account (e.g., Chrome on Windows 7 or Android-based device). If you notice any unfamiliar devices or locations, you can end the session by clicking on the "End Activity" button.

Login notification—enable your Facebook login notification so that you can be notified through e-mail or text message when your account is accessed.

> ➢ *Steps:* Login to your account → "Account Settings" → "Login Notification" → "E-mail" and/or "Text."

The notification e-mail provides detailed information about the login, including the IP address used, location, time, and type of device used to access the account.

Disable or revoke third-party apps—Your information (e.g., friends list and profile) is available to third-party applications (or apps for short) running over Facebook. Third-party apps are developed by people other than Facebook, but have access to Facebook. While third-party apps improve your Facebook experience (e.g., if you allow access to the Wordpress app, your Facebook updates will automatically appear on your wordpress.com blog), some of them may be vulnerable to attacks or may handle your account information insecurely. Here is how to disable the vulnerable apps.

> ➢ *Steps:* Login to your account → "Account Settings" → "Security Settings" → "Apps" → "Edit" → "Disable Platforms."

Use strong passwords—to protect your Facebook accounts from hacking always use a strong password. See the strong password guidelines discussed earlier. Strong passwords are difficult to hack or guess.

Securing Your Twitter Account

Use login verification—like Facebook, Twitter also provides two-mode authentication known as *login verification*. After enabling the login verification feature, you will need both your password and your phone to log in to your Twitter account. When you log in to Twitter.com, you will receive a text message with a login code or a push notification.

> ➢ Steps: "Settings" → "Security and Privacy Settings" → "Send login verification requests to my phone" → when prompted, click "Okay, send me a message"→ if you receive the verification message, click "Yes."

Before using this feature, make sure that you verify your e-mails, add a phone number, and check that your carrier is Twitter-supported. Instructions on how to confirm your e-mail address is provided here: https://support.twitter.com/articles/97942

Revoke third-party apps—Like Facebook, Twitter also provides access to third party apps. While these apps makes your Twitter experience more convenient, as mentioned earlier, some of them may be vulnerable to attacks or may handle your account information insecurely. Here is how to disable them.

> *Steps:* Log in to your account → "Settings" → "Apps" → you will be provided with a list of apps that have access to your account → "Revoke Access."

Use strong passwords—to protect your Twitter account from hacking, always use a strong password. See the strong password guidelines discussed earlier. Strong passwords are difficult to hack or guess.

Securing Your Blog

The following are some techniques to secure your blog.

Two-mode authentication—*Steps* Go to your blog and click on your avatar (or profile picture if you have uploaded one) available in the upper right-hand corner of the window → "Account Settings" → "Security" → "Two-Step Authentication."

Disconnect third-party applications—**Steps:** "**Account** Settings" → "Security" → "Connection Applications" → click on any unwanted applications that you want to remove → "Remove App Connection."

Back up your blog—You can back up your blog's content (including posts, pages, comments, custom fields, terms, navigation menus, and custom posts), which then can be restored in case of emergency. Here is how to do it.

Step 1: Go to your blog by typing its address into your Internet browser.

Step 2: Click on the "WP Admin" option. This will bring you to the blog's "Dashboard."

Step 3: Once in the Dashboard click on the "Tools" available at the lower left corner of the dashboard, and then on "Export." There are two export options: "Export" and "Guided Transfer." Select the "Export" option.

Step 4: You will be offered a "Choose What to Export" option. Click on the default "Select All Content" and click "Download export file." Save the file in a secure location. It can be restored when needed.

To restore the blog content you have exported earlier, use the following steps.

➢ **Steps** "WP Admin" → "Tools" → "Import" → from the available systems select "WordPress" → "Choose the file" you have saved to your computer → "Upload file and Import."

Use strong passwords—to protect your blog accounts, always use a strong password. See the strong password guidelines discussed earlier. Strong passwords are difficult to hack or guess.

Dual authentication can also be applied to other social media platforms, including wikis and YouTube.

RISK EVALUATION

Social media risk management is a continuous process. In the face of rapid technological, political, and social change, social media risks should be periodically reviewed. Your risk-management strategy, procedures, and techniques should be continuously updated in response to the emergence of new social media platforms, social changes, and potential new risks. The continuous evaluation and monitoring effort will make sure that the initial assumption made about the external and internal risks are still relevant.

Review Questions

1. What is the goal of aligning social media analytics with business goals?
2. Explain the social media alignment matrix.
3. Briefly explain the role of CIO in aligning analytics with business objectives.
4. What is the purpose of social media strategy?
5. Explain the steps needed to formulate a social media strategy.
6. What are some common social media risks?
7. Explain the four steps in social media risk management.
8. Explain common social media risks-mitigation strategies.
9. Explain different techniques to secure social media accounts.

REFERENCES

Ackland, R. (2010). WWW Hyperlink Networks. Analyzing Social Media Networks with NodeXL: Insights from a connected world. D. Hansen, B. Shneiderm and K. H. M. Smith, Morgan-Kaufmann.

Agarwal, A., K. Hosanagar, et al. (2011). "Location, Location, Location: An Analysis of Profitability of Position in Online Advertising Markets." Journal of Marketing Research **48**(6): 1057-1073.

Bekmamedova, N. and G. Shanks (2014). Social Media Analytics and Business Value: A Theoretical Framework and Case Study. the 47th Annual Hawaii International Conference on System Sciences, IEEE Explore.

Berners-Lee, T. (1993). The World Wide Web Initiative, CERN, available at: http://www.ncl.ac.uk/computing/research/seminars/pdfs/chapters/92.pdf.

Biuk-Aghai, R. P. (2006). Visualizing Co-Authorship Networks in Online Wikipedia. Communications and Information Technologies, 2006. ISCIT '06. International Symposium on.

Bjorneborn, L. (2001). Necessary data filtering and editing in webometric link structure analysis. Royal School of Library and Information Science.

Björneborn, L. and P. Ingwersen (2004). "Toward a basic framework for webometrics." Journal of the American Society for Information Science and Technology **55**(14): 1216-1227.

Boyd, d. m. and N. B. Ellison (2007). "Social Network Sites: Definition, History, and Scholarship." Journal of Computer-Mediated Communication **13**(1): 210-230.

Burt, R. (1992). Structural Holes: The Social Structure of Competition. Cambridge, MA, Harvard University Press.

Chakrabarti, S., M. M. Joshi, et al. (2002). The structure of broad topics on the Web from http://www2002.org/CDROM/refereed/338

Chakraborty, G., M. Pagolu, et al. (2013). Text Mining and Analysis: Practical Methods, Examples, and Case Studies Using SAS, SAS Institute.

Chen, H., C. R.H.L., et al. (2012). "Business Intelligence and Analytics: From Big Data to Big Impact." MIS Quarterly **36**(4): 1165-1188.

Chen, Z., F. Lin, et al. (2002). "User Intention Modeling in Web Applications Using Data Mining." World Wide Web **5**(3): 181-191.

Dawes, S. S. (2008). What Makes a Successful CIO? Intergovernmental Solutions Newsletter, GSA Office of Citizen Services and Communications. **21**.

Editorial (2014). "Editorial Expression of Concern: Experimental evidence of massivescale emotional contagion through social networks." Proceedings of the National Academy of Sciences **111**(29): 10779.

França, U., H. Sayama, et al. (2015). "Visualizing the "heartbeat" of a city with tweets." Complexity: n/a-n/a.

Garrido, M., & Halavais, A. (2003). Mapping networks of support for the Zapatista movement: Applying social network analysis to study contemporary social movements. Cyberactivism: Online activism in theory and practice. M. M. M. Ayers. London, UK, Routledge.

Garvey, P. R. (2008). Analytical Methods for Risk Management: A Systems Engineering Perspective,. Boca Raton, London, New York, Chapman-Hall/CRC Press, Taylor & Francis Group (UK).

Ginsberg, J., M. H. Mohebbi, et al. (2009). "Detecting influenza epidemics using search engine query data." Nature **457**: 1012-1014.

Hanneman, R. A. and M. Riddle (2005). Introduction to social network methods. Riverside, CA, University of California (published in digital form at http://faculty.ucr.edu/~hanneman/).

Hecht, L. (2013) "Location Analytics: The Future is Where."

Henderson, J. C. and N. Venkatraman (1993). "Strategic alignment: leveraging information technology for transforming organizations." IBM Syst. J. **32**(1): 4-16.

Hofstede, G. (1984). "Cultural dimensions in management and planning." Asia Pacific Journal of Management **1**(2): 81-99.

Hofstede, G. (1991). Cultures and Organizations: Software of the Mind. London, McGraw-Hill.

Hunt, C. (2014). "Social Media Ownership: Recommendations for Employers, available at: http://denovati.com/2014/02/social-media-ownership ".

Jackson, M. H. (1997). "Assessing the Structure of Communication on the World Wide Web." Journal of Computer-Mediated Communication **3**(1): 0-0.

Kaplan, A. M. and M. Haenlein (2010). "Users of the world, unite! The challenges and opportunities of Social Media." Business Horizons **53**(1): 59-68.

Kaplan, R. S. and D. P. Norton. (2001). "The Strategy-Focused Organization, available at: http://iveybusinessjournal.com/topics/leadership/building-a-strategy-focused-organization#.VLjEetKUd5E."

Khan, G. (2013). "Social media-based systems: an emerging area of information systems research and practice." Scientometrics **95**(1): 159-180.

Khan, G. F. and S. Vong (2014). "Virality over YouTube: an empirical analysis." Internet Research **24**(5): 629-647.

Khan, G. F., H. Y. Yoon, et al. (2014). "Social media communication strategies of government agencies: Twitter use in Korea and the USA." Asian Journal of Communication **24**(1): 60-78.

Kielman, J. and J. Thomas (2009). "Special Issue: Foundations and Frontiers of Visual Analytics." Information Visualization **8**(4): 239-314.

Kietzmann, J. H., K. Hermkens, et al. (2011). "Social media? Get serious! Understanding the functional building blocks of social media." Business Horizons **54**(3): 241-251.

Kim, D. and Y. Nam (2012). "Corporate Relations with Environmental Organizations Represented by Hyperlinks on the Fortune Global 500 Companies' Websites." Journal of Business Ethics **105**(4): 475-487.

Korf, M. and E. Oksman. (2014). "Native, HTML5, or Hybrid: Understanding Your Mobile Application Development Options, available at: https://developer.salesforce.com/page/Native,_HTML5,_or_Hybrid:_Understanding_Your_Mobile_Application_Development_Options."

Kramer, A. D. I., J. E. Guillory, et al. (2014). "Experimental evidence of massive-scale emotional contagion through social networks." Proceedings of the National Academy of Sciences **111**(24): 8788-8790.

Latapy, M., C. Magnien, et al. (2008). "Basic notions for the analysis of large two-mode networks." Social Networks **30**(1): 31-48.

Liu, X., J. Bollen, et al. (2005). "Co-authorship networks in the digital library research community." Information Processing & Management **41**(6): 1462-1480.

Luftman, J. N., C. V. Bullen, et al. (2004). Managing the Information Technology Resource: Leadership in the, Information Age, Prentice Hall

Lustig, I., B. Dietrich, et al. (2010) "The Analytics Journey: An IBM view of the structured data analysis landscape: descriptive, predictive and prescriptive analytics." Analytics-Magazine, available at: http://www.analytics-magazine.org/november-december-2010/54-the-analytics-journey.

Marsden, P. V. (2008). Network Data and Measurement, London: Sage.

McAfee, A. P. (2006). "Enterprise 2.0: the dawn of emergent collaboration." MIT Sloan management review **47**(3): 21-28.

Minch, R. P. (2004). Privacy Issues in Location-Aware Mobile Devices. the 37th Hawaii International Conference on System Sciences, Big Island, HI, USA.

MITRE. (2014). "Risk Impact Assessment and Prioritization, available at: http://www.mitre.org/publications/systems-engineering-guide/acquisition-systems-engineering/risk-management/risk-impact-assessment-and-prioritization."

Nam, Y., G. Barnett, et al. (2014). "Corporate hyperlink network relationships in global corporate social responsibility system." Quality & Quantity **48**(3): 1225-1242.

Niven, V. (2013). "Does Purchase Intent Exist in Social Media? avilable at: http://www.needtagger.com/does-purchase-intent-exist-in-social-media/#qHHu5pCZMYCpPP05.99."

Nooy, W. D., A. Mrvar, et al. (2005). Exploratory Social Network Analysis with Pajek (Structural Analysis in the Social Sciences) New York, Cambridge University Press.

Oreilly, T. (2007). "What is Web 2.0: Design Patterns and Business Models for the Next Generation of Software." Communications & Strategies **1**: 17.

Pan, B. (2015). "The power of search engine ranking for tourist destinations." Tourism Management **47**(0): 79-87.

Pan, B., H. Hembrooke, et al. (2007). "In Google We Trust: Users' Decisions on Rank, Position, and Relevance." Journal of Computer-Mediated Communication **12**(3): 801-823.

Park, H. and M. Thelwall (2008). "Link analysis: Hyperlink patterns and social structure on politicians' Web sites in South Korea." Quality & Quantity **42**(5): 687-697.

Park, H. W. (2003). "Hyperlink network analysis: A new method for the study of social structure on the web." Connections **25**(49-61).

Perer, A. and B. Shneiderman (2008). Systematic yet flexible discovery: guiding domain experts through exploratory data analysis. 13th Int'l Conf. on Intelligent User Interfaces, New York, USA, ACM.

Petersen, R. (2012). 166 Cases Studies Prove Social Media Marketing ROI, BarnRaisers.

Preis, T., H. S. Moat, et al. (2013). "Quantifying Trading Behavior in Financial Markets Using Google Trends." Sci. Rep. **3**.

Ransbotham, S. (2015) "Once You Align the Analytical Stars, What's Next?".

Shulman, S. (2014). "Five Pillars of Text Analytics, available at: http://www.screencast.com."

Simon, S. J. (2000). "The impact of culture and gender on web sites: an empirical study." SIGMIS Database **32**(1): 18-37.

Straub, D. W. (1994). "The Effect of Culture on IT Diffusion: E-mail and FAX in Japan and the U.S." Information Systems Research **5**(1): 23-47.

Syncapse (2013). THE VALUE OF A FACEBOOK FAN 2013: Revisiting Consumer Brand Currency in Social Media. New York, NY

Thelwall, M. (2001). "Exploring the link structure of the Web with network diagrams." Journal of Information Science **27**(6): 393-401.

Thelwall, M. (2005). Webometrics. Encyclopedia of Library and Information Science M. A. Drake. New York, Marcel Dekker, Inc.

Thelwall, M. (2014). Big Data and Social Web Research Methods University of Wolverhampton, available at: http://www.scit.wlv.ac.uk/~cm1993/papers/IntroductionToWebometricsAndSocialWebAnalysis.pdf.

Vaughan, L. (2004). "Exploring website features for business information." Scientometrics **61**(3): 467-477.

Vaughan, L. and M. Thelwall (2003). "Scholarly use of the Web: What are the key inducers of links to journal Web sites?" Journal of the American Society for Information Science and Technology **54**(1): 29-38.

Vaughan, L. and J. You (2006). "Comparing business competition positions based on Web co-link data: The global market vs. the Chinese market." Scientometrics **68**(3): 611-628.

Vreelnad, R. (2000). "Law libraries in cyberspace: A citation analysis of world wide web sites." Law Library Journal **92**: 49-56.

W3. (2015). "What is Linked Data? available at: http://www.w3.org/standards/semanticweb/data."

Wal, T. V. (2005). "Off the Top: Folksonomy Entries, avialable at: http://www.vanderwal.net/random/category.php?cat=153."

Wasserman, S. and K. Faust (1994). Social network analysis: Methods and applications. Cambridge, Cambridge University Press.

Wasserman, S. and K. Faust (1994). Social Networks Analysis: Methods and Applications. Cambridge, UK, Cambridge University Press.

Webber, A. (2012). Guarding the Social Gates: The Imperative for Social Media Risk Management, available at:http://www.slideshare.net/Altimeter/guarding-the-social-gates-the-imperative-for-social-media-risk-management, Altimeter.

Weideman, M. (2009). 2 - Elements of website visibility and research. Website Visibility. M. Weideman, Chandos Publishing**:** 41-58.

Wong, P. C. and J. Thomas (2004). "Visual Analytics." IEEE Computer Graphics and Applications **24**(5): 20-21.

Yalçin, N. and U. Köse (2010). "What is search engine optimization: SEO?" Procedia Social and Behavioral Sciences **9**: 487–493.

Zhang, J. and A. Dimitroff (2005). "The impact of webpage content characteristics on webpage visibility in search engine results (part I)." Inf. Process. Manage. **41**(3): 665-690.

Glossary

A

actions, 4, 10, 40, 41, 43, 46, 52, 57, 107, 113

actions analytics, 4, 40

Ads oriented apps, 54

Airbnb, ix, 56, 57

alerts, 81, 94, 107, 108

alignment, 101, 103

always-on, 55

Amazon *CloudSearch*, 91

analyzing networks, 33

Anderson Analytics, 8, 9, 10, 12

API, 8, 5, 12, 13, 30, 60, 62, 85

API based extraction, 8

app development, 56

apps analytics, 52, 53

Apps analytics, 52

Assess Your Organizational Culture, xi, 106

association mining, 6

Autofill Columns, 37

Average bounce rate, 41

average degree, 28, 29

B

Betweenness centrality, 28

Blogs, 5, 114

Brandwatch, 13, 14

Bucket option, 87

Business data driven location analytics, 80

Business data-driven location analytics, 79

business insights, 4, 6, 7, 9, 1, 2, 5, 6, 21

business intelligence, 4, 10, 1, 3, 5, 41, 62, 80

business objectives, 1, 6, 7, 101, 103

C

carriers, 60, 61

Centre for Social Technologies, 35, 72

Challenges to Social Media Analytics, 10

Check-in, viii, 42

CIO, 104, 106

classification, 6, 42

Cleaning stage, 8

clicks, 41

clustering, 6, 8, 6, 21, 28, 31, 33, 35, 37, 80

clustering coefficient, 28

Co-authorship network, 24

Co-commenter networks, 24

co-likes networks, 24

co-links, 66, 68, 69

Co-links, ix, 67, 68, 102

collaboration, 7

Collaboration and Sharing, 80

comments, 1, 3, 4, 6, 8, 9, 10, 2, 5, 1, 2, 3, 4, 6, 8, 11, 12, 15, 23, 24, 29, 32, 37, 40, 42, 70, 76, 101, 108, 116

Components, 29

Concept mining, 5

Content communities, 4

Content networks, 23

content strategy, 107

Content strategy, 108

conventional analytics, 3

conventional business analytics, 2

conversation, 2, 7, 13, 3, 2, 29, 46, 102

Core Characteristics of Social Media, 2

Countly, ix, 1, 11, 56, 57, 58, 59, 60, 61, 62, 63, 64, 102

T

U

Made in the USA
Charleston, SC
23 June 2016